CEO SPEA

"Real wo...

This internationally acclaimed series provides real world lessons from C-level business leaders (CEO, CFO, CTO, CMO, Partner) of some of the world's most respected companies. Each chapter is a future-oriented look at the most important issues for success. Every contributor has been carefully chosen for his or her proven business expertise in order to give readers actual insights from the thoughts, perspectives, and techniques of accomplished professionals worldwide. Because so few books or other publications are actually written by executives in industry, this series presents an unprecedented look at contemporary issues never before available.

"What C-Level executives read to keep their edge and make pivotal business decisions. Timeless classics for indispensable knowledge."
Richard Costello, *Marketing Communications, General Electric*

"Unique insights into the way the experts think and the lessons they've learned from experience." MT Rainey, *Co-CEO, Young & Rubicam/Rainey Kelly Campbell Roalfe*

"A great way to see across the changing marketing landscape at a time of significant innovation."
David Kenny, *Chairman & CEO, Digitas*

"Unlike any other business book."
Bruce Keller, *Partner, Debevoise & Plimpton*

"A must read for those who manage at the intersection of business and technology."
Frank Roney, *General Manager, IBM*

CEOs on Business Success

Top CEOs Reveal the Secrets of Management, Market Leadership and Profits

VISION BOOKS

(Incorporating Orient Paperbacks)
New Delhi • Mumbai • Hyderabad

www.vision**books**india.com

Authorized edition for sale in the
Indian Sub-continent and South-East Asia

ISBN 81-7094-589-5

© Aspatore, Inc., 2001
All rights reserved
Originally published as *Leading CEOs*
www.aspatore.com

Published in 2004 by
Vision Books Pvt. Ltd.
(Incorporating Orient Paperbacks and CARING imprints)
24 Feroze Gandhi Road, Lajpat Nagar-III,
New Delhi-110024, India.

Phone: (+91-11) 2983 6470 ; 2983 6480
Fax: (+91-11) 2983 6490
E-mail: visionbk@vsnl.com

Cover Design by hatchdesign.org

Printed at
Rashtra Rachna Printers
C-88 Ganesh Nagar, Delhi 110092, India.

Contents

Fundamentals Never Go

Out of Style

Frederic M. Poses

American Standard Companies

Chairman and Chief Executive Officer

Back to Basics

The business world's myopic infatuation with the "New Economy" has cooled. The dot-com bubble has burst. The record ten-year expansion of the U.S. economy has officially ended, and the world economy entered 2002 in what was looking like a classic global recession, complicated by international tensions.

None of these conditions is welcome, but neither are they cause for panic. They amount to a reminder that economic cycles are still very much part of business life. Tough times also reinforce a valuable management lesson: Fundamentals never go out of style.

Consistent attention to the fundamentals of your business will help you minimize the damage in difficult economic times and make your company stronger and more competitive when the business cycle turns around. It's been my experience that managers who are on top of the fundamentals of their business are also on top of the shifting patterns in their industries. They are generally better able to anticipate changes in the marketplace, to "see around the corner," and to act with the speed and flexibility to take strategic advantage of what they see.

When I think about the fundamentals of a successful business, I have three major concerns:

- *People*: Are we recruiting and retaining the best possible talent and giving our people maximum opportunity to develop and expand their skills and increase their value to the company?

- *Environment*: Are we creating the kind of working environment where people are results-driven, where expectations are high, and where the organization is structured to help people achieve results?

- *Focus*: When the economic cycle eventually turns down, do we keep our perspective and stay focused on the basics of growth-building, such as improved customer service, competitive new products, and the kind of operating efficiency that supports profitability?

The People Factor

People are your pivot point. Any graduate business school program will emphasize the importance of strategic and operating plans. Those plans, though, are only as good as the people you select to implement them. Recruiting and keeping talented people is the real art of management. A successful company is built around people who can deliver and execute – people who understand a company's vision and can turn it into action that pleases customers, motivates co-workers, and creates value for shareowners.

You can't know with certainty what the company or the world will look like ten years – or even ten months – from now. Instead of relying on predictions, you have to rely on people in your organization with' the talent to change the company as the world changes. Building a successful company requires people who are open to change, not just for the company but for themselves. Some very talented people will not survive organizational change because they themselves will not change. They are in yesterday's paradigm, which held them in good stead yesterday, but is a bad fit today and a disastrous career trap tomorrow.

Ultimately, business is a game in which you choose the best players and work the game plan or fundamentals to help them win. It's not a game of solitaire; it's a team sport. You have to give people the opportunity to get into the game and use both their technical and their interpersonal skills to make a difference.

It comes down to creating an open environment where people feel free to share and take risks, are encouraged to excel, and can expect to be rewarded for succeeding. That's a prerequisite of a good leader, and a priority for any CEO in identifying good leaders within a business.

Leadership takes passion, commitment, boldness, and self-confidence, qualities innate in leaders. You can build on and improve these qualities, but my feeling is that either people have them or they don't.

A real leader creates an open environment by being consistently open to the ideas of others. Nobody has an answer for every question or a solution for every problem. As CEO, I may be responsible for a decision, but I know my decision will be better if it reflects the best thinking of the right people in our organization.

I have probably learned more from people who have worked for me over the years than from my bosses. By nature I am an observer – a listener and a watcher. The idea is to learn from others, but not to impersonate them. As a leader, I have to learn from others and then connect what I've learned to my own passions and convictions.

Communication is a critical skill for a leader. You must communicate your vision, passion, and desire to win if you expect people to follow you. Your message also has to be consistent. If your message today is "March north," and tomorrow it's "March east," after a while, people will get confused and won't respond.

You need a vision you can articulate with consistency. Consistency has taken a bad rap as the "hobgoblin of little minds." In organizations, consistency is a welcome alternative to chaos. When leaders change within a business, a new leader might have a strong desire to make changes that are inconsistent with the role, strategy, or values that employees have been urged to accept in the past. If you have to break with the past, make sure people understand why. Without that kind of communication, they will understand only that their organization is without consistency, and it's a quick jump from there to feeling they lack leadership.

Communication also creates enthusiasm. It's a way to motivate and teach. For example, we write a letter once a month to our employees about some topic of common interest. It could be about speed or safety. It might encourage our employees to think about what they contribute to the company. We send out a letter quarterly on how we are doing financially, and we made a global satellite broadcast recently to employees in one of our divisions to talk about a transition we are making. You also can communicate by doing things as simple as walking the halls or walking the factory floor. Just imagine being able to talk to every employee every day in person to swap ideas and concerns. You would certainly have a better company.

It is rare that a manager builds a new team from the ground up, with entirely new players. You almost always start with some existing players who've been with the company for a significant amount of time, in some cases longer than their leader has. Chances are high that you have some substantial talent in this group of veteran players, and it's an important part of your team-building responsibility to recognize and develop the talent of these veterans. These people will bring vital continuity to your efforts if you also take on the challenging job of blending them effectively with the new talent you recruit to enhance or add skills and experience.

Assembling a great team, though, is just the beginning of your responsibility as their leader. Once you've identified your team, you have to make sure they can work together and stay focused. The better the team is, the more motivation and support they need from their leader. To keep good people on a team, keep challenging them. As you retain your good people by giving them challenging and meaningful work, your team develops a reputation that will make it easier for you to recruit more good people in the future. So a virtuous circle is created.

Creating the Right Environment

There's an endless list of variables that can help create the environment that helps people excel, including a good cafeteria, a fitness center, an on-site daycare center, varied benefit choices, and a reward system that includes stock options. Beyond those tangible things, though, you have to create an environment that provides people with a framework in which they strive for success. A framework like that has to include high expectations.

High expectations of achievement – for both individuals and groups – are essential to a thriving, growth-oriented organization. High expectations drive innovation, and innovation means change. If you have modest expectations, then your incentive is to work just a little harder to reach them. You won't change your fundamental approach very much because you'll probably ask the same questions of the same people and get the same answers and results. High expectations, by contrast, create an environment where people realize they can't get where they want to go by doing business in the same old way. That sets the stage for innovation.

It's been my experience that innovative ideas spring from interaction within small groups, rather than from an individual. To demonstrate, try a simple exercise. Write down your solution to a problem, and then brainstorm with your colleagues. I guarantee you will come out with a much better solution after conferring with them. High expectations bolster innovation and promote cooperation.

High expectations, translated into definable goals, also create their own discipline. They give people a framework for making decisions. If you have no idea of your leader's goals for the business, you have no basis for setting your own work priorities. You cannot be disciplined in what you do. Self-discipline occurs when people have a clear idea of what the leadership of the company expects from them.

It's also important to carefully target expectations and goals. If a company's leadership identifies 47 goals, an individual or team couldn't possibly develop the discipline to meet them all. But if people are asked to focus on three important goals, then they have the flexibility to move left or right, backward or forward, depending on opportunities. They can ask, "Which of these moves will get me to goal one, goal two, or goal three?" Given the right combination of clear expectations and operating freedom, people will be self-disciplined as they produce results.

Finally, it's important that employees have their own high expectations and set individual goals that align with those of the business. If employees appreciate and understand a company's expectations, they should develop their own expectations for helping the company achieve its goals. If you want them to set their expectations high, make it clear the company understands and embraces the need for risk.

Risk-taking is sometimes mistakenly viewed as taking part in something dangerous. To me, there's nothing more dangerous than trying to do things the same way year after year. Taking too few risks or none at all only creates a bigger risk that a competitor will beat you.

As a leader, you have to see the value in trying new ways of doing things, support your team in their efforts, and accept that there will be wins and misses. Risk-taking, by definition, comes without a guarantee. Your job, then, is to encourage risk-taking while effectively managing risk. It's part of your responsibility in growing the business.

Managing risk is a skill you develop through experience. I've learned over time to focus on those projects or ideas that are risk-worthy. You can measure risk-worthiness by asking the classic question of whether the reward is worth the risk.

For example, I once worked for a company that created a stain-resistant carpet. At the time, the idea was risky because we didn't know if we had the technology to produce it, if we could get the customers, or if there would be a high degree of warranties involved. But the biggest risk was that no one had ever done it before. It was uncharted territory.

Yet we realized that if we succeeded, we could turn a commodity fiber into a branded fiber and sell it for a lot more money, making it a risk-worthy project. So we took risks: Would the innovation work? Could we market it? Would the customer pay for it? The product succeeded and more than vindicated our risk-taking. It was a win, and everybody likes to win.

We did plenty of things that were risk-worthy but didn't win for us. So our approach to risk-taking is like building a batting average and accepting that we will strike out now and then. Of course, a company cannot afford to undertake 20 high-risk projects at the same time because the likelihood of success is relatively low. It's important to maintain a balanced portfolio of high-, medium-, and low-risk ventures. Too many long shots with no returns waste precious resources.

When you choose to take a risk, you should evaluate that risk all the time. Measure the odds every day because they change, whether the risk is on a person, a new product, or a customer. Just because you took a risk and got on the road with it does not mean you should stay on that road. Sometimes you have to accelerate risk-taking and at other times, pull over and stop. Most people don't stop early enough when a risk begins to look bad. Hope is no substitute for reason. Unfortunately, people keep hoping for the outcome they want, even when the evidence is telling them it won't happen.

Good companies take risks, but when the risk goes against them, they minimize their losses. It's like being a trader: Good traders play the upside and minimize the downside. They get out early enough to avoid a catastrophe. That's how you effectively manage risk, but it's a hard decision for a leader to make.

You will always have people who desperately want to move forward with a project. Their passions are engaged, and their rewards might depend on it. But sometimes a leader must say, "Enough is enough." Don't tell people they have failed, because failure creates an environment in which people are too afraid take risks again. You want to avoid that. Rather, a leader should help people understand that knowing "when to fold 'em" is an important part of managing risk.

When your company's leadership shares its vision with its employees, empowers them to act, and gives them the skills and tools they need, you create a formula to win. But you need to measure your progress against your goals, communicate your progress, and keep your employees focused on achieving those goals.

As a leader, you have the important responsibility of selecting the appropriate metrics. Any single metric in its own right doesn't give you an accurate measure of performance. You have to link metrics together. For example, you cannot look at sales growth without profit growth. Sales growth is an important characteristic of how well you are doing with customers, but it is not good enough. Or you can measure inventory turns, but you need to measure lead times, too. If you promise delivery in two weeks and then take four weeks, you're not doing a good job even though your inventory turns might be phenomenal. If you invest time in developing a meaningful measurement process for all major activities, it will pay off handsomely in increased efficiency.

As a starting point in analyzing your performance, look at your competitive position in your industry. If you are growing sales above and beyond others, it must mean you have the products, the marketing, and the service to be winning with customers – a good top-line indicator. Now, that top-line performance will be different in good versus bad times, but in any economic climate you can measure your success by measuring your top-line performance against that of your competitors. But don't fall into the trap of getting so enamored with your top-line performance that you neglect your bottom line.

If you have a lot of top-line growth and no bottom-line growth, you are just worshiping at the altar of market share without getting its rewards. Ask yourself, "Am I improving my fundamentals?" In a softening economy, you might not be making as much money as you were before, but if you are doing the fundamental things that make a good business, you will have progress to measure. Those fundamentals include buying better raw materials, producing better products with fewer defects and higher quality, and introducing new products. Don't make the mistake of easing up on measurements until the business climate improves.

At the American Standard Companies, we've made it clear that we have three constituencies: customers, employees, and shareholders. That's been our mantra from day one. We constantly ask what we are doing for those three groups.

It is easiest to communicate with shareholders. We set specific goals for growing our top line, our earnings, and our free cash flow. That is something our shareowners can understand. If we communicate it as our long-term goal, they can measure us each year. We believe that when we deliver on those goals, our shareholders will be rewarded with an increasing stock price.

For our customers, we simply ask ourselves, "Do we have the products? Do we have the services? Do we have the delivery time? Overall, are we becoming a more preferred supplier today than we were yesterday?" If the answer is "yes" to each of those questions, we'll see sales growth.

To our employees we owe opportunity. This means an opportunity to grow with the company, either by being promoted and having a different job, or by enhancing their ability to contribute more by learning and using new skills. We provide our people the opportunity to do that. It is their responsibility to take advantage of it. Those employees who take advantage will be more successful, have greater opportunity and, in an uncertain world, have greater job security.

So I keep my eye on three things. First, I closely follow the pace of our business and how we are doing with customers. Second, I'm concerned with how well we manage talent. I ask, "Are we helping our people get better? Are we recruiting and retaining new talent?" And third, I keep my eye on our stock price. While on any given day our stock price is not a perfect barometer of how we are doing, in the long term it is an objective measurement of how many people want to buy our stock and how many people want to sell it. If we are doing a good job, then the demand will be higher than the supply, and the price will go up, so investors are the ultimate judge of our performance.

Staying Focused in Difficult Times

Difficult times don't mean you throw away your proven strategies and start casting around for miracle cures. In good times or bad, the fundamentals of the game do not change. You have a strategy; you have customers; and you have to execute.

It's always important to keep business cycles in perspective, but that's contrary to human nature. When the economy is good, people have a tendency to believe it will continue to get better indefinitely. When the economy looks grim, some of the same people convince themselves the situation will never turn around. So in tough times, you know pessimism will rise to the surface. You need to counter it with a vision that says, "We have good businesses. We have good people. We will do the right things. And the market and our business will turn around."

It's both motivating and reassuring for employees to hear that the best way to combat tough economic times is to dig in and work even harder on the same fundamentals we worked on in good times. Conditions might demand we work a little differently. In difficult times, flexibility is your best defense against uncertainty. The market can slide away from you more quickly, so you want to react faster. And when the market picks up, you want to be the one who can take advantage first. So speed and flexibility are at a premium.

You can still make money in difficult times – in fact, you are paid to make money. Someone will sell products, and someone else will not. Our job is to be the one who sells, perhaps not as much as we would have sold before, but more than our competitors sell. Often that means creating new products that stimulate sales. You can also take advantage of weak supplier markets during difficult times to control your costs. For many companies, the toughest thing about tough times is realizing you often have to work harder for smaller rewards. If you do that, though, you will be in a stronger position to grow faster than your competitors when the economy begins to improve.

There is always a weak competitor out there – someone who does not have the new products, the distribution, the cost structure, or the customer trust that they will make it through the difficult times. If you are a customer, you will go with the one you think will be there for you today and tomorrow. It is interesting that bad economic times can also make you into a better business. When business is booming and your product lines are chronically sold out, you don't have the inventory or the motivation to create new products and services that sweeten your total offer to customers. But the improvements you make in bad times can significantly improve your fundamental position with customers and against competitors.

In good economies or bad, successful selling begins with understanding the fundamentals of your industry. The fundamentals of our industry say that many sales opportunities don't come around more than once. If I missed the sale today, I have missed the sale forever. If I miss the sale of a commercial air conditioning system today, I'm not going to recoup by selling two systems to the same customer tomorrow. It's a little bit like selling newspapers: If you don't buy today's newspaper from me, I can't make it up by selling you today's newspaper tomorrow.

Once you understand the fundamentals of your industry, you have to understand the timing of when your customer will come back. If an air conditioning unit breaks in the southwestern region of the U.S. in October, we know the customer might not replace it until March, when it starts to get warm. So that demand will come in six months. We have to be ready to sell when the customer is ready to buy, to understand his timing and be ready when he is.

Understanding the fundamentals, understanding your customers, and having the speed and flexibility to react truly distinguish companies that succeed in difficult times from those that miss the turn. They miss the turn on the way up because they don't understand the fundamentals of their own success. And they miss the turn on the way down because they don't understand the fundamentals of what's wrong with their business.

Keep Working the Fundamentals

Business fads come and go. Products and technology change. But the fundamentals of the game aren't all that different today than they were at the start of recorded commerce. In the year 2002, winning revolves around the fundamentals of finding customers, creating the value customers want, and delivering that value with enough efficiency to make money doing it. And I suspect things won't be very different when this new millennium comes to a close in another thousand years. That's why it's so important to have people in place who can change the company as the world changes.

Frederic M. Poses is the chairman and chief executive officer of American Standard Companies, Inc. Before joining American Standard, Mr. Poses was president and chief operating officer of AlliedSignal, Inc. He joined AlliedSignal as a financial analyst in 1969 and was named general manager of the company's Home Furnishings Division in 1977. From 1977 to 1988, he held several positions of increasing responsibility and was appointed president of the Engineered Materials Sector and executive vice president of the corporation. In October 1997 he was elected to the board of directors and named vice chairman of AlliedSignal, Inc. He was appointed president and COO in June 1998. Mr. Poses spent two years on assignment in Peru with the Peace Corps before joining AlliedSignal. He holds a BBA from New York University. He serves on the board of directors of the 92nd Street Y and is a member of the board of trustees at the Riverdale Country School.

High-Tech Company, High-Touch Values

John W. Loose

Corning

President and Chief Executive Officer

Getting to Know Your Business

It was very helpful to me, over the years, to be exposed to every business in the company I work for, Corning, and getting to touch every business and actually work in it. I started in the consumer products business, but then moved around to a variety of our operations and had the benefit of gaining many different points of view. I tell my kids, who are young adults, that I am a big believer in getting a broad variety of experiences in your 20s, 30s, and early 40s, as opposed to thinking of your career in rifle-shot terms.

In my own career I took three lateral moves. From a tactical point of view, the benefits weren't always clear at the time. But from a broadening point of view, it was great. I have always argued for gathering a wide variety of experiences. In this company, those opportunities are everywhere because this is a multi-business company – television glass, optical fibers, liquid crystal display, catalytic converters. I encourage people to get exposed to as many facets of the company as they can, to get a different kind of functional experience and fresh perspective.

Setting the Operating Environment

My management style is based on some of my basic beliefs about the best ways to do business. First, it is very important to be sure you are locked onto a strategy. I am always questioning and challenging the assumptions that have helped us to arrive at all of our strategies.

It is also important to believe in the customer. I think one of the great strengths of Corning is its technical base, its science, and its remarkable record in life-changing inventions. The great thrill is seeing these technologies come out of the research, into development, and finally into the marketplace. With this in mind, it is crucial for me to talk to the organization about that important linkage between technology and the marketplace.

Often in technology companies, there is interest in technology only for its own sake. The technology crowd is out in its own orbit or sphere; it's not well connected to the customers in the marketplace. It's not that way at Corning. Whenever I go to the lab at Corning, I always ask the scientists several questions: When is the last time you saw a customer? What is the customer saying? What are you learning about the marketplace? Where is the marketplace going? Are you working on projects that will allow us to make a quantum leap in terms of where technologies of markets are going?

Another important aspect of good management style is focusing on the set of values of the company. Corning has seven values that are not very different from those of other successful companies. So you have to figure out what makes you truly different. What we look for is an operating environment – or a set of behaviors – that articulate exactly what those values look like. It states very clearly and specifically how we can most effectively do our work and work with one another. Here are the principles of our Operating Environment:

- We work together as a global team.

- We value and respect each other.

- We drive innovation and discovery.

- We deliver superior customer value.

- We commit to achieve excellent results.

- We move quickly from idea to customer.

When we review people annually, we use these statements as a measurement. Individuals get feedback from their leaders and their peers on the extent to which their behavior is aligned with the operating environment. We also run employee surveys to measure how well the overall work environment is aligned with the operating environment.

Making It Personal

I am also a big believer in communication. It's become my style to spend a lot of time communicating with the organization. In tough times, it is particularly important to communicate to everyone within the organization. More importantly, the CEO must do the communication, not send others to convey the directions of the company. For example, it became very clear to me six months ago that you couldn't send committees out to communicate with the organization, that I had to do it myself. With a lot of help, we put together a program where once a month I send a personal e-mail to virtually every employee in the company. It serves as a vehicle for them to write me back, ask questions, and comment on what I am saying – and believe me, they do. We answer their questions or put them in contact with people who can answer. It really helps form a personal contact – this is hard because we have more than 30,000 employees.

I can't see everybody, but I try. Every six weeks, I do a sort of road show. I go into an auditorium with as many 500 people, and I sit on the stage, make some comments for ten minutes, and answer any question anyone wants to ask me. We give everyone an index card when they come in. While I am doing my pitch, it will prompt them to think of things, and they write down questions. Then the cards are collected and brought to me. You would not believe the stack of cards I get, and they leave nothing in the bag. People ask very plain-talk questions because it is safe.

I think I'm getting good marks for being out front and talking to the organization, and I move these meetings around. I provide a steady diet of voice mails, as well – always after we announce financial results because we want people to hear the news from us first. We use voice mail, too, during emergencies. It was a very important way for us to communicate with everyone following the tragedies of September 11.

Avoiding the Bogey Man

Business problems may be different during downturns in the economy, but the approach to working on those problems really isn't very different. First I look at the data, or the facts. I have always said that with 100 percent of the facts you can generally figure out any problem. Unfortunately, you cannot typically get 100 percent; you may get 80 percent, and from there you just have to use good judgment.

As CEO, after examining the data, I have to figure out the best move and then get that decision into motion. I am generally data-oriented, so I make fact-based decisions. I am probably known for being very rigorous from a process point of view. I walk through the issue and do what I have to do. Once I know I have a good, fair process in place, I move quickly.

More importantly, as you work on solving a problem, the CEO has to continue to talk to people about what is happening and why, and whether the company's performance is going up or going down. The big difference during challenging times is that leaders have to get out in front of the organization – be there physically. When times are tough, the people in an organization can get discouraged. They are worried they'll lose their jobs. The anxiety of not knowing where a situation may lead breeds a lot of stress. I try to acknowledge that by talking to them and giving them facts. One of the big problems in these situations is what I call the bogey man syndrome – people make up stories and start rumors when they don't have facts. The most important thing we can do is keep talking, getting the message out, and at least getting the bogey man off the table.

Building a Company to Last 100 Years

A successful employee has to be bright – has to have some good, innate process skills and decision-making skills. Because Corning was a family-run company for many years, people are well grounded with their values, and their values are consistent with what this company stands for.

We look for a special kind of human being. Corning looks for people who are here for a solid, growing career. We look for leaders. We recognize there are individual performers, and there are leaders, and individual performers are just as valued. In fact, the patents of intellectual property come largely from individual performers – the underlying strength of the company.

One of the biggest responsibilities of a CEO is to make sure we have people in place who can lead this company into the future. With my staff, I spend a lot of time on career development. If we have 15 people in their 30s and 40s who we think can lead the company in the future, we decide what to do to help them develop in their careers.

As you can imagine, it is very gratifying to be the CEO of a 150-year-old company. More importantly, we are a 150-year-young company. How have we survived all this time?

I think, when we look back on our history, the answer is in our DNA. Corning is unique in that it is very comfortable with big technology bets, and it's also comfortable being patient with its money. We spent years perfecting optical fiber before we made any money. We had hundreds of millions of dollars in losses in the LCD (liquid crystal display) business before we made any money. We are very comfortable making these big, home-run, technical bets, and they are industry-changing bets. When I talk about telecommunications, one of our big ideas is we think telephone networks are going to run on protons, not electrons. We believe LCD will replace the CRT (cathode ray tube), and we know how to do it. We are very comfortable in capital-intensive businesses, so a big, capital-intensive factory development does not make us uncomfortable. The payoffs are huge when you have proprietary technologies that are game-changers.

But you have to be very rigorous. This continues today and is certainly part of my responsibility. You have to be rigorous about your portfolio and know when it's time to cut and run. In the 1960s, when I was coming into this company, 65 percent of the company was devoted to television. Color television was the hottest item in consumer products; color TVs were starting to get bigger, get into the bedroom – it was an unbelievable market. Profits were pouring in, and it was great. Today it is an asterisk, and we have methodically exited the television business. We've made a bet on television glass over in Korea with our joint venture there – Samsung Corning – but we have basically backed away and invested in other technologies, such as LCD and telecomm. We invented the glass casing for the electric light bulb – and now, we are basically out of the lighting business. Lighting was the business this company was founded on – the basis of the company 100 years ago – but we are out of it now.

As with most companies that have lasted 100 years, this company is continually transforming itself. We watch the life cycle of businesses very carefully; we believe in it. You make your money in the growth stage of the life cycle. When you start going over the top of the life cycle, and it's getting mature, profits start to shrink. Then you get into decline, and it's over. We work very hard to anticipate when products will start coming over the top and then make plans to move on and reinvest in other types of technologies.

Managing Risk to Maximize Opportunity

To manage risk, basically, we have a rigorous innovation process. We're as risk-averse as anyone else. Everyone wants a sure thing. On the other hand, we are a technology company founded on innovation. We have a five-stage innovation process, and it starts with ideas.

Think of a funnel, with a billion ideas going into the back of the funnel. Assume 300 go in – and one comes out the other end. Obviously you want to shave those 300 down as fast as you can, because, otherwise, it's a waste of money. So we go through this idea stage, with a checklist. The next stage is determining whether the idea is feasible. Following the feasibility stage, an examination determines whether it is practical. Then there's the pilot line, and finally commercialization.

Before we can go from idea to feasibility, there is a long checklist of technical, commercial, and financial questions that need to be answered. It is not meant to kill every idea, but if it becomes obvious that an idea will never see the light of day for whatever reason, we will kill it. The same process occurs for each stage. This is a very rigorous process, which is essential and important to us.

For example, a high-profile project we were working on this year was a technology to put down on a glass slide 10,000 dots of DNA. Every dot would be a different dot of DNA. We had developed a technology to do it and were testing it with MIT. We loved the performance of the product. It worked better than anything on the market, but we killed it. We killed it because it couldn't get through the practicality stage gate. The business model we had was not consistent with the marketplace. We had an open architecture market and, simply put, we had the product to put the dots down, but we didn't have all the software that ran it. The competition was selling a closed-architecture product, a turnkey sort of deal, which is what the customers want. We were not prepared, didn't think we could invest the money, and didn't have the capabilities. We are not a software house, and we killed the project. It was a good decision. Obviously we will save a lot of money going forward, and we kept ourselves from spending a lot of money when failure was probably inevitable.

Challenges and Choices for a CEO

Having grown up in all of our businesses and being from the operations side, one of my biggest challenges is being the CEO and not the COO.

The CEO role is fascinating. The early challenge for me was dealing with the investment community. I learned you deal with the investment community as you deal with everyone else. You're open; you tell them what you can tell them; and you don't surprise them. It's the way you want to deal with anyone. Your integrity is the most important asset you have with the investment community; everything you do has to be oriented around protecting that asset.

Another challenge that, I think, probably all CEOs face is the touch of loneliness at the top. I think you just have to recognize that and know that the relationships you had in the past will be different when you become a CEO.

A challenge for me is that I, a fact-based kind of decision-maker, can never get 100 percent of the facts. I once got some advice to take the 80 percent I can usually get, and go with my gut. It works. You'll be right 90 percent of the time, and with the other 10 percent, you won't gain much anyway.

The advice I usually give others is to relax. Normally, when people come into my office, they are keyed up about something or some crisis of the moment. I always try to tell them to slow down, and let's just deal with it: What is the data? What are the facts? Let's not shoot any messengers. Let's choose to deal with the challenge objectively, not blame anybody, and just work our way through it.

Looking into Leadership

A lot of the qualities of leadership come naturally. In my own life, I was a leader on the playground; I was a quarterback in college. I have always been very comfortable with leadership, and I do think there is some natural essence in leadership. But you can truly move forward as a leader by making yourself learn. I spend a lot of time on my own personal development. I am a great believer that we're always learning. I think that's important in all individuals.

You should never typecast anyone, and never say a person has leveled. Don't generalize about people. I find that people are remarkable; some are early bloomers and fade early, and some are late bloomers and blossom late. This was true for me: I was a very late bloomer. I was a sales guy for ten years, and people thought I would be a sales manager one day. I got some breaks, though, and blossr ied late. It has been my experience never to typecast people and never to generalize about what a person can and cannot do. You must give everyone a chance to succeed and, equally, a chance to fail.

I think a lot of the fundamentals of management will change in the future. The piece I see changing the most is the move of more organizations toward team leadership. More and more, you see executive teams at the top of the company, rather than the traditional hierarchical type of organization that was typical in the past. Leading a high-level executive team presents some it own challenges because you are dealing with people who are accomplished and smart and who already have a track record. There are also different personality styles among the team members – another set of challenges for leadership.

John W. Loose joined Corning in 1964 and through 1985 held a variety of sales and marketing management positions in the Consumer Products Division. In 1985, he was named vice president and general manager-Asia Pacific. Three years later, he was named vice president International, Corning Incorporated, and president and chief executive officer of Corning Asahi Video Products Company. He was subsequently named senior vice president-International, Corning Incorporated.

In 1990, Mr. Loose was named executive vice president, Information Display Group and became president and chief executive officer of Corning Vitro Corporation in 1993, which became Corning Consumer Products Company in February 1994. In 1996, he was named president-Corning Communications and co-chief operating officer of Corning Incorporated, which included worldwide responsibility for the Telecommunications Products Division, Siecor Corporation, the Photonic Technologies Division, and Corning International.

Mr. Loose was named president and chief operating officer in December 1999 and became chief executive officer of the company in January 2001.

Serving on the board of directors for Corning Incorporated, Dow Corning Corporation, and Polaroid Corporation, Mr. Loose is also a trustee of the Corning Incorporated Foundation and the Corning Museum of Glass. He is a member of the Business Council, the Business Roundtable, and the Business Council of New York State.

Mr. Loose holds a BA degree from Earlham College and completed the Program for Management Development at Harvard Business School.

Balancing Priorities for the Bottom Line — Employees, Customers, Shareholders

Bruce Nelson

Office Depot

Chief Executive Officer and Chairman

Foundation of Trust

The most important foundation for anything, but especially a business, is a foundation of trust. This trust must translate itself later into confidence. Trust is being as open and forthright as possible and as truthful as possible in every situation. In my business I try to be direct, to hold confidences, and to have no hidden agendas. That is how I manage, and that is the basis on which I build business.

Dialogue is essential because it creates opportunities for disagreements because of the responsibility to express different viewpoints blended with facts and opinions. Facts and opinions are important considerations in decision-making. They combine with intuition to form the basis for all major decisions. Dialogue means there is room for healthy disagreements, not disagreements for disagreement's sake, but to reach a better decision. When the disagreement ends, there must be unanimity.

The process must be highly participative. I never make a key decision without input. I want input sometimes to reinforce a decision already made or if I need different ideas and viewpoints for discussion. I am pragmatic in that the end result should dictate the approach.

I have a philosophy about bottom lines and people, but people should never be ignored; sometimes decisions need to be made that put people ahead of profits. This might contradict what shareholders want, but creating loyalty and a friendly environment where the employees like to work is more important than the shareholders' views.

Employees must always know where they stand. A manager must be clear with expectations and tell people if they need to improve their performance. The challenge of executives is to keep in touch with those who do the work, who really understand what is happening in a business – the employees.

When assembling a team of employees, strive for an eclectic group. Not everyone should be the same, with the same background and education. An effective team must be diverse in every way, such as in age, gender, and race. This will complement the diversity of the management team that brings different business experiences and life experiences to the business. The management team must be diverse in its views to complement the employees' diversity.

Great leaders are not distinguished by sheer brilliance, but rather by a combination of reasonable intelligence with understanding and empathy for people and the human condition. A team must strive to work in a synergistic way, in that their group effort is greater than the sum of the efforts of the individuals on the team. That is based, again, on the concept of trust that inspires open dialogue among the members of a team. When the leader is the only one who brings out the issues, always having to criticize and commend, the team functions less effectively than it could if peers spoke up. Teamwork is more effective when peers speak to peers.

I try to encourage relationships between my workers, professional and otherwise. They need to trust each other. There is always conflict; conflict must be addressed with dignity, with no hidden agendas. Different viewpoints must be aired in different ways. Some people express themselves more assertively, while others are better listeners.

Leaders must always listen and look for the subtleties. The obvious about a certain employee or situation is easy to see; what is underneath is often more important. Essentially the "underneath" deals with cause and effect; often the effects are the issues.

Working in Harmony

Management and the employees in a business must work i harmony with each other, directly and forthrightly, toward mutual trust and dignity. Being part of a team means no exclusivity. There is no room for favoritism in a team. The team's concerns come before the concerns of individuals. As an owner of a business I want my employees to speak loudly about the state of their units, but I also want to them to be able to step back and say, "What is the best thing for the whole – not just the particular pieces?" Promoting such openness and honesty in dialogues requires employees who are empowered to act and speak on behalf of their beliefs.

Employees need to be empowered to feel empowered, as illustrated in the difference between entrepreneurs and corporations. An entrepreneurial spirit gives an individual the freedom to initiate, respond, and create. Entrepreneurs can be creative, responsive, and quick to adjust to change. I want my decision-making to mirror this entrepreneurial spirit. It is essentially authority with limits. Limits are not the same for everyone because people have different abilities and experiences. I try to set up freedom within a defined set of boundaries. When an employee grows beyond the boundaries, I will expand the boundaries for that particular person accordingly. It is important to allow them freedom in decision-making, but not to the point of isolating them. Thus, empowered employees develop over time through experience.

Recognition, rewards, and actions become the indicators of an empowered employee. Learning stems from mistakes, so the CEO needs to determine where it is safe for employees to make mistakes. Sponsoring empowered employees lies in the subtle, day-to-day workings and letting the employees have the measured autonomy and freedom to make decisions that may differ from the decision I would make in the same situation.

To become a leader in more than title, a CEO must have an inner drive that comes from deep inside. It must be more inside than outside. Many people are motivated extrinsically – by a bonus check, a new car, for example. I think to be a true leader, you must have intrinsic motivation. To be a really great leader, you must have an insatiable appetite for accomplishments and results. You must always want to get better. That is a motivation to grow, to learn, and to convert this growth into action.

Great leaders are able to judge, coach, evaluate, and teach others. Great leaders replicate themselves. They are great selectors of talent. They can grow talent, nurture it, and reap its benefits. Great leaders are great with people. Leaders must also understand fully what they are leading. Leaders need to have a fire in their belly, a burning passion for what they do, and the ability to do what they love.

Leadership has its costs. Not everyone likes a leader – that sounds easy to deal with, but it is hard to value respect over someone's approval. To lead a large corporation means sacrificing weekends, relationships, and time. Everything has a cost.

Responsibilities of a CEO

The first and most constant responsibility faced by a CEO is to sell his or her vision for the company and the future of the company. This always varies according to audience.

Relating to Wall Street is a matter of personal involvement in investor conferences, in conversation with major holders, in approaching the market of institutions and preaching the vision as an ambassador, a visionary. It is telling all these people, in all these settings, why your business is a compelling place to invest. That is the hands-on, personal touch that is needed to convince.

Top leadership follows a similar approach when communicating within the company. It is easier for a CEO to have contact with two levels of the organization – the people who report directly and those who report directly to them. I know them and contact them often. I spend an enormous amount of time with them individually and in groups. This face time builds confidence and trust.

When elaborating on these principles for larger groups, we must use modern means – for example, sending videos out once a month to my 40,000 Office Depot employees. We require our managers to see me on video. These videos are memos from the CEO. On our Web site is a link entitled "Ask Bruce." I do not personally respond to all questions, but many times I do. I read my own e-mail and respond often. I send many emails.

I alert our employees to whatever our company does in the public eye, such as what we give to charity. The CEO must communicate well and often. Sometimes this necessitates saying the same thing over and over in different ways. When I became CEO, I developed a mantra that was simple and easy to remember: "I want Office Depot to be the most compelling place to work, shop, and invest." I used that mantra over and over. We use videos, face time, letters, and memos to tell people there is a vision and that the leadership is open, willing to communicate, and trustworthy. This ultimately persuades them to buy into the vision. If they buy into the vision, their output will be enormous. It creates a synergistic energy: Magic happens

The Three Focuses of a CEO

The three main day-to-day focuses of a CEO are people, money, and customers. People are affected through human resources; money is managed through the CFO; and customers are managed through marketing. The CEO needs sufficient data about all three. I examine the data based on its type, particular to the situation.

When dealing with people, I look for loyalty, turnover rate, progression rates, diversity, promotions, litigation, and how the litigation is resolved. I read the annual surveys. I see how leaders are developing and whether they are developing others. I look at whether the bulk of the people resources are internal or external.

When dealing with cash, I look at the cash in the bank, the balance sheets – not all of them, but enough to get an insight. If more is needed, I look for more. Some numbers will raise a flag, and these numbers demand my attention. To me, a good CFO is like a giant flashlight on numbers that illuminates the dark corners.

When looking at customers, I look for new customer growth, customer complaints, customer trends, and why complaints end up on my desk without being stopped before they get to me. I look at answer time, response time. I look at 15-20 indices daily. Based on what I see or sense, I may take the data further.

There needs to be a blend in priority of people, money, and customers. Ideally, they complement each other.

In the next ten years, claims for a CEO's time will grow more demanding. Externally, the shareholders will want more face time. If your business is part of a community, then it is expected to be more civically active. If the company is a major employer, it must participate in political and social issues, such as educating children. The CEO is always pressed to join a board to help raise money for certain issues. Internally, people want more access to the CEO. The workforce changes. It is far different than it was, say, 15 years ago. Employees are not as loyal in that they demand more leadership and change.

There are many variables now that must be considered by a CEO running a business. In the future that number will only increase. CEOs in the future will deal with more complexities. There are social, economic, political, and international variables, and the CEO must understand all of these. Technology's effects on business are difficult to keep up with, and global communication makes more information available to more people. Then the CEO must distinguish between information and data. Computers can give me information, but I have to determine what information I need to manage. With more information, there is less time for the essentials.

You can overcome these challenges if you have an appetite to grow and convert learning into practice while focusing on results and accomplishments. On top of this, you must still balance short- and long-term results. Today there is more pressure for short-term gains, rather than long-term development. That is a problem of the American free enterprise system. Stockholders are becoming more and more demanding. Being a CEO means juggling time, complexity, and political, social, and economic issues, then integrating all these pieces, fitting them together as a whole.

Managing Change and Risk in a Fluctuating Economy

When analyzing the company's position, the CEO must try to balance or harmonize short-term goals with long-term goals. It may mean sacrificing short-term gratification for long-term results. You have to step back and say, "I want this company to withstand the test of time, and to do this it must be able to change and adapt." The external environment changes and adapts; competition changes; the economy changes; social needs change; and the workforce changes. A company must change, and to be a leading company, it must lead the change. This means being willing to change directions, attitudes, and cultures and being willing to sacrifice the now for the later.

Difficult, uncertain times call for heightened pragmatism in business. You must focus on cost escalation. You don't have as much freedom as you have in good economic times. You must use more discipline and be more aware about adding cost and resources. Realistically, this should be a constant, but tougher times call for more rigor and discipline.

The time frame is shorter, creating a sense of urgency for decision-making. Your management team must ask where the company will be next month, rather than setting up a two-year plan. The CEO must also pay more attention to small trends – even weekly and monthly trends. A boom economy allows you to look further out into the future when making decisions. Managing through these cycles creates an ability to see using the short-term perspective rather than long-term, particularly if the company is publicly held. You tend to be more critical as a result of this sense of urgency. You want to inspire more from employees.

Revenue growth is the first thing to suffer in an economic downturn. The reality is that you have to put far more focus on cost in a short period than during an expanding time. You must be more concerned with escalating costs, adding costs, and, overall, deferring costs. When facing capital expansion, you must ask, "What will another month cost?" Or, if someone wants to hire a new executive, you must ask, "Why not wait a month or two? Why must this issue be addressed immediately?" Decisions become much more heavily focused on cost and quality. This can be a blessing: By focusing on quality and customers in lean times, you can gain more consumer loyalty for the good times. Tough times inspire more change.

From a customer perspective, a customer company might think of making changes during an economic downswing that it would not have thought about in good times. You must take advantage of these times, in the sense that quality and service must be the last qualities to suffer. This, allows the company to gain an advantage – customer loyalty – from a stressful time. In that regard you must start by identifying costs you can change: "What costs can I take out of my business that are furthest from the customer?" The closer the changes are to the customer, the more caution you must exercise.

During economic downturns, where change is inevitable, it is important to position your company to withstand the changes and allow for flexibility in management. Someone once told me humans (and organizations) are more resistant to change when things are going well than when they are going poorly. When a company is succeeding, in good times and bad, change is more of a challenge because people will be blind to the changes they need to make. It is easier to improve a company when it is not doing well because the need for change is clear. A crisis must be handed to you, or you have to create one.

Great leaders can create crises to inject a reason for change. In a difficult economy it is easier to pinpoint what is not working and change that. It is effective to assemble employees who have the most contact with the customers and ask them how their company can change. This will improve customer loyalty and employee loyalty. This gets back to company culture. If a company recognizes, cajoles, forces, and rewards change, it will be more likely to change. Creating a need for change is difficult because a company is an organizational culture from people to systems to measurements, and humans are inherently resistant to change.

When changes must be made, risks will be undertaken. When mitigating risk, you must determine whether the risk is substantial enough to wager the whole company on one decision. You must be extremely cautious and rarely gamble this much. To make a decision regarding risk, you must assess the size of the risk and know the upside and the downside. It is the magnitude of the risk that determines what decisions are made. It is always proportional. If the budget calls for capital expenditures of $300 million, and someone has a viable $10 million idea, this idea is, for all practical purposes, worth the risk. If it is a $40 million idea, more research and thought are needed. Look at analysis, insight, rationale, market competitive data, and some analytics, and then examine some opinions. There is also a subjective aspect; you must ask, "How does this feel?" Then it is time to say, "Let's do this," or "Let's not do this."

These decisions are always made in the context of six or seven people. I never make a decision without my CFO, or without the business owner who has the risk. It is not always consensus, but I want them to have an understanding of the total picture. They must understand the risk fully before making a decision.

There is always a sponsor of the risk. The sponsor could be the CEO in acquiring something or moving in a direction, or the risk may be from a business perspective, but people need to be held accountable for taking the risk. If I call an authority to measure a risk and it works, I will have more confidence in that person's judgment. Risk is always relative to its size and impact, as well as the size of the bet and the size of the return. Making the decision depends on an analytic aspect and a gut-check quality.

Overall the CEO must remember the difference between people and the bottom line. I had mentors who said you must always look at both. I could never be a slash-and-burn leader. To me, leading is about people, the value of people to a company. As leaders we react to others. Someone once told me that when I have a strong reaction to an individual – another leader, a manager, whoever – I should hold the mirror up and look at myself because my reaction is often a reaction to myself. I call this "insight into oneself." I do not think you can have insight into others unless you have some insight into yourself.

I have been fortunate to work for people who have taught me the quality of being aware. Be aware. It sounds too simple. A number of years ago I acquired some companies on behalf of a Dutch company I ran here in the U.S. I wanted to give them plaques for their desks. They were supposed to be engraved with the words, "Be Aware." The printer made a mistake, though, and the plaque read, "Be Ware." I was asked whether I meant one or the other, and I responded, "Yes." You must always be aware and beware.

Too often leaders cut themselves off from reality – that is, the truth of what is happening – and this isolates them and causes them to make bad decisions when they face risk in an ever-changing economy. You must always listen and engage yourself. That is being aware enough to understand where the truth really is and exist in an environment where the truth can be brought. I work hard to foster an environment where my employees will not feel the messenger will be shot. The awareness of the CEO will inspire the trust of his or her employees, which will make managing the company easier and give the CEO a better sense of the company's future well-being when making decisions regarding risk.

Bruce Nelson began his office products career in 1968 with Boise Cascade Office Products in Itasca, Illinois. During his 22 years with Boise, he held a variety of senior management positions in both the wholesale and the contract business segments.

From 1990 to 1994, Mr. Nelson served as president and chief executive officer of BT Office Products USA, where he led

BT's rapid U.S. expansion into the contract stationer segment through an aggressive acquisition program.

In January 1995, Mr. Nelson joined Viking Office Products as executive vice president. He was named chief operating officer the following year, and in January 1996, he was promoted to the position of president. In November 1996, the shareholders elected Mr. Nelson a member of the Viking Board of Directors. With the merger of Viking and Office Depot on August 26, 1998, he was appointed president and chief executive officer of Viking and president of Office Depot International; and he was elected to the Office Depot Board of Directors. In July 2000, he was appointed chief executive officer of Office Depot.

Active in variety of industry associations, Mr. Nelson serves on the board of the U.S. Chamber of Commerce and the CHARLEE (Children Have All Rights, Legal, Educational and Emotional) Foundation, an organization established to assist abused and neglected children in the foster care system in Dade County, Florida. In addition, Mr. Nelson has held other industry leadership positions, including with the BPIA (Business Products Industry Association) and the City of Hope. In 1994, he received the Anti-Defamation League's Office Products Industry Man of the Year Award, and in 1998, he received City of Hope's highest honor, the Spirit of Life Award.

Keeping the Right People

in Your Company

Thomas C. Sullivan

RPM

Chairman and Chief Executive Officer

Picking Proper People

The right people are hard-working people who have fun. You can trust them. They have a great deal of integrity in their own personal habits, as well as in dealing with the people around them. Because of RPM's reputation for having a small, entrepreneurial management team, a lot of people were attracted to us. That gave us a great advantage in attracting individuals from some of the support firms that are now working for us. For example, Steve Knoop, who is currently in charge of RPM's acquisition program, actually came from our general counsel, who worked with me on acquisitions. Steve Knoop made the comment that he did all the work and wasn't able to stick around for the fun of growing and watching the businesses grow.

I have also met many wonderful, fine young people through my four sons. I talked to them when they graduated from business schools, and fortunately, I was able to persuade some of them to join RPM. We've had very little turnover here. It's just a great group of people.

The key way to keep good people with your company is to be honest with them and with yourself from the outset. Most histories of acquisitions are filled with horror stories. The biggest obstacle of an acquisition is overcoming the stories "out there" that never worked. With RPM, we generally practice what we preach. And we say, "If you're working and doing well, we'll give you plenty of incentives." Many of those incentives are based on how much our operations earn. They can be unlimited, including stock options and running your own company. That formula has worked extremely well for RPM. And it continues to do so, and that's why we haven't lost people.

What tips you off that you have the right person for a job is knowledge about their performance and how they handle themselves. I can guarantee that you can't interview somebody over two or three days and figure out whether they are going to be the real thing. We have been fortunate that good people have been attracted to us through some of these outside providers, as well as through people some of my children knew. Five or six of our top management people today came into RPM, Inc. within two years of one another after writing us letters saying they'd love to do nothing more than work at RPM. So we have been very lucky at the corporate level.

On the operating level, you have something you just don't have in an interview: You have a history of a company to look at, which provides a picture of the makeup of its people. If you're looking at a company that has performed extremely well in its marketplace and has a management team that has been working together for a long period of time, you can see that this team is going to continue together. All that you have to do is provide that atmosphere. Picking people at the operating level is a lot easier than picking them for the corporate level.

Becoming a Business Leader

There is no set formula for becoming a leader in business. Different people lead in different ways. You have to be very comfortable in what you are doing, like what you're doing, have integrity, and work hard. I do think it's that simple. I was a B student and am probably one of the few in my company who don't have a master's degree. I nearly flunked chemistry. I wasn't the greatest student. After college, I was a communications officer aboard a destroyer in the Navy for a couple of years. At the tender age of 23, I had 60 men under me – some were kids, and others were older than I was. And I was told they were my responsibility. Every young person who wants to grow up to be a leader should have a similar experience. To know how to lead, you first have to learn how to follow. I think you have to understand that.

To keep a company moving in the right direction, we have offered and given tremendous autonomy to companies that we have acquired. You could be looking at 20 individual units, which are actually operating as part of one RPM in the coatings industry. Because we broke the larger entity into smaller units, it's much easier to manage its growth. Growing a $100 million company to $500 million in the next five years is much more meaningful than growing a $2 billion company to $5 billion over the same period. It's the way we have broken down our operations into smaller units and put each of those operations on annual planning. Although we look at stretch plans over a three- to five-year period, we have very good control over an annual plan, and that's essentially how we operate.

Management Basics

As CEO, my most important responsibility involves communicating our strategies to both our people and the financial community. Along with that responsibility is ensuring that our operations take advantage of the synergies among them, since they're all essentially part of the same industry. Then, it's basically waving the flag.

To wave the flag at RPM, it is essential to focus on our two constituencies: our shareholders and our employees. After that, I then encourage our operating people to go out and serve their customers. I think it would be nearly impossible for RPM, Inc. to be customer intimate; so that's left to the various operational units. Obviously, we have to be conscious and aware of the needs of the major companies in the consumer area, principally the mass merchandisers.

To manage successfully through all sorts of turbulence in the economy, it is important that management doesn't swing and sway with what is happening to the economy. RPM has had 52 consecutive record years in sales and earnings. I became CEO in 1971, when we were an $11 million company. It grew from that point for 32 consecutive record-setting years in sales and earnings, and we managed through some severe raw material shortages, the hyperinflation of the 1980s, and about four major recessions, including the one we're in now. With the exception of the last two years, the results out of that period were all good. In fact, now we have had 54 consecutive record-setting years in increased revenues, and in all but one of those 54 years, we increased earnings year after year.

We position our smaller units to thrive on change in the marketplace. RPM is not in the position to drive any of the operations. We provide them with incentives to do a good job.

When RPM, Inc. acquired Rust-Oleum in 1994, it was a specialized, small-package, rust-inhibitive coatings company that owned its market. One of its well-known competitors decided it would try to expand its market from the general and decorative small-package paints position and go after the rust inhibitor. They were advertising on TV, and my thought was, "Uh-oh. We may have acquired a company that that came with more competition than we expected." The people at the operating level – the Rust-Oleum people, not the RPM people – said the way to combat this is to go after the general and all-purpose market. Today, Rust-Oleum is better than three times the competitor's size and controls a good majority of the broader all-purpose, decorative, spray-in, small-package market. Basically, this success was achieved though category management, where the top people at the operating level made the adjustments and made a better situation out of adversity.

To plan, a CEO must try to set realistic goals. Back in the 1980s, we were telling everybody we wanted to see their growth at double-digit levels. Back in the 1980s, we also had inflation that was 6 percent to 8 percent, so that goal was more meaningful. Inflation in the 1990s kept our internal growth somewhat below the mid-single digits. We told our operations they could get to double-digit growth with our help by adding product lines through acquisitions. We've been able to maintain that trend throughout the 1990s, even though there was no inflation during that period.

To set goals and put the company in an advantageous position to reach those goals, a CEO can look at the plan in two different ways. First, it is the CEO's responsibility to try to figure out where the company will be in five years. From 1971 to 2001, we were very accurate in plotting the goals of RPM, Inc. to essentially double ourselves every five years. Along with that, you have to figure out what you're going to need in that process in terms of corporate support and what you're going to need at the operating level in terms of their support. You then tell the operating people, "OK, keep this five-year goal in line, but we want to hear from you only on a 12- to 18-month plan. Give us something in 12 to 18 months that correlates to what we are doing, but something you can do." Then we give them strong incentives to make that happen.

And it has happened for two reasons: We have picked only good companies to acquire from the start, and we kept our promise to give autonomy to good management. We never felt we were smart enough to do turnarounds. So we've picked very good companies, some of which I had been following for up to 20 years before they joined RPM.

By putting the growth down into the smaller units, increasing sales annually on a continual basis doesn't look like impossible. Then of course, growth also includes acquiring companies; acquisitions have accounted for about half of our growth over that 30-year period. So the combination of managing down, in the sense of having our smaller operations be a part of the growth planning process, and making select acquisitions has proved successful for us in a consolidating industry.

Valuing a Company

When looking at an outside company, you obviously put a financial value on a company that has much to do with what they will bring to you in terms of growth on the bottom line. Then, it is important how the company is positioned with its customers – whether it's broad-based throughout North America or global.

Another key aspect in valuing a company is how it is positioned within its own markets. It's putting all of those things together and then putting a multiple on it. Of course, the management team is also an important element in valuing a company. My company never goes after an acquisition candidate where the management team does not stay to work with RPM. And we've been very fortunate; we've lost very few managers who have come to RPM.

When to Hold 'Em, When to Fold 'Em

Managing execution is done best through the planning process. Our operations are tracked on a monthly basis. At RPM Inc., we receive a profit and loss statement and a balance sheet for every operation we track. Watching how they execute is simple. When they don't execute, we walk in and give them some help. In very few cases have we replaced management that has failed to execute for one reason or another.

In a couple of cases, we have sold businesses because the markets have changed on them. Markets generally change from specialized to commodity. And RPM, Inc. simply can't work with commodities under our operating philosophy. So in the extreme, we have sold businesses, and in some cases, we have changed management to make sure we are getting the proper execution.

As for execution at the corporate level, it's a very wide-open-door policy. We certainly have the lines of responsibility and authority necessary in any business, but I think a lot of us keep our eyes on everything – particularly the details. That's a way of ensuring execution.

Although RPM, Inc. has restructured once in 30 years (resulting in the end of 52 consecutive years of record earnings), there are others ways to restructure without going through some of the pain you have to endure in an announced restructuring program. Moreover, there are smarter ways you can restructure over longer periods of time. By taking care of business on an annual basis, you don't get yourself into a position where you have too much capacity in your manufacturing and don't know what to do with it.

Encouraging Innovation

Innovation in a company often comes in terms of new products because they drive any company. The people at RPM, Inc. are all aware of that. At RPM, we have the advantage of our consumer people looking at some unique industrial products and saying, "I can take this into my distribution." So we have products that are unique and different to the consumer level. The interplay of technology within our own organization brings along a lot of product innovation.

Beyond that, we push innovation back down to the operating people. Most product innovation that comes in our industry starts at the marketing and sales level. In some cases, innovation is talked about at the customer level before we get involved in changing things and doing things that are innovative.

Handling Risk in Acquisitions

You take a risk every time you make an acquisition. To manage that risk, you build up a trust with those you work with in the acquisition world.

I have always been at the front line in acquisitions. Now we have a whole staff for that purpose, led by Steve Knoop. We have built up all of these people with the idea that when we go out there and sell our story and our philosophy, things tend to become a little bit easier.

To reduce further risk in acquisitions, we have some very fine support people, including outside lawyers, outside accountants, and outside environmental people. These support groups all conduct due diligence and report back to us. We ask the companies we are going to acquire to be open with us. We need to trust one another because many people will go in and verify for me the various aspects of what we have been talking about. When you go through this process over a long period of time, you develop a huge group of people who have a great trust in what you are doing and can work with one another to achieve a unified vision.

Invaluable Advice

My father gave me my best piece of business advice when he said, "Go get good people; create the atmosphere that will keep them; and let them do their jobs."

Another piece of great advice I received was from Bill Karnes, who was chairman and CEO of the $4 billion Beatrice Foods. That company was a true conglomerate that everybody followed and admired. At the time, we were building a new corporate office building for a group of vice presidents. I had a great deal of enthusiasm for this plan. After telling him all about it, Karnes looked at me and said, "Tom, you're doing it all wrong." He said you have to be as close to those operating presidents as you can, and you don't want to build a layer in between them. After hearing that, I scrapped all those plans, and interestingly enough, we don't have a group of vice presidents today.

Other great advice I've received came from the three wonderful directors that were on RPM's board: Les Gigax, retired president of Rubbermaid; George Karch, retired chairman of the old Cleveland Trust, the largest bank in Ohio at the time; and Niles Hammink, who just retired as chairman of Scott and Fetzer, which is now a part of Berkshire Hathaway. After reaching our first $100 million in 1979, I was the happiest guy in the world. The company had proved to itself and to a lot of other people that it could grow. To celebrate this milestone, we had a huge party. After that party, those three gentlemen came to my office, sat down, and said, "For the last time, congratulations. Now we are going to tell you what you are doing wrong."

George Karch said, "You brought in some acquisitions that were good, but they're not good now, because their margins have shrunk. You have to get rid of them. It's the bottom line that counts, not the top line." Les Gigax said to me next, "Tom you have a five-year plan for RPM – that's neat. Nobody has an annual plan for the operations. Here's

Rubbermaid's annual plan. Pick the best of this. But get your operations on a plan." Then Nile Hammink gave us the real wisdom. He said, "You have a bunch of entrepreneurs running around that could care less about Tom Sullivan or Jim Karman or RPM, Inc. What you've got to do is get these people cooperating with one another. Tom, you've got to stop acquisitions and work on this." That's when Jim (now RPM vice chairman) was made president in 1978. I turned over all the details to Jim and the planning to Jay Morris (now retired executive vice president). I worked only on long-term acquisitions issues. That advice built RPM to what it is today.

The advice I give most often to others is to be honest with yourself and with those around you, and believe in yourself. Integrity is the most important thing you can have. If you do enough, you're going to have a few failures. If you don't have any failures, you're not doing enough.

To deal squarely with failures as a CEO, you have to take responsibility for them. Don't try to pass responsibility for them on to other individuals or other things happening. Stand up first and say, "It happened on my watch. It was my responsibility." If you don't do that, you'll lose good people. When you take responsibility, people recognize that at least you're trying. Moreover, if you've done something that's failed – and my father taught me this a long time ago – it's okay; just don't fail twice at the same thing. Look at what happened; recognize it's a failure; determine why it failed;

learn from it; and move on. Don't have a long memory with failure.

Maintaining Your Edge

I read when I can, to stay current. More often than not, I count on my people. A little more than a year ago, they put a computer on my desk. My secretary of 40 years came in and said, "You press this button and it turns on." I e-mail people back and forth, but I still get out of my desk and go talk to people. I think that's how you monitor the pulse of your business and motivate your people. They know you have a personal interest in them, and they know you're interested in having them do a good job too. I think all of that gives people some confidence. You have to give people a pat on the back and say, "Good job." Sometimes that goes further than a pay increase.

You need a well of people to build a company that will last. Products will change a hundred years from now, and I wouldn't even attempt to guess what our products will be a hundred years from now. There may be substrates out there that don't need paint. I started in this business mixing chemicals in a drum with a wooden paddle. We've advanced greatly from there, but this isn't a hi-tech industry.

The only area we've ventured into that was considered mechanically hi-tech is rubber roofing. It became a commodity and was a huge mistake for RPM, Inc. We lost a lot of money, but we managed our losses and got out of it finally. We were one of the first into it with Gates Engineering. Then Firestone decreed it was rubber – it may be roofing, but it was rubber – and decided they were going to get into it. They took the price from 70 cents to 17 cents per square foot, and it ruined that business for us.

We've also gone through the e-commerce bit in the last couple of years. Our e-commerce department had up to 14 people. We dismantled much of that, though, because we found we're not selling quite as much off the Web as we thought we would. What the Web has done for managing our systems and things of that nature is absolutely beautiful. We are doing a lot of architectural specs, but not much direct selling.

Keeping that well of good people relates to the founding philosophy my father had: Get good people; create the atmosphere to keep them; and let them do their jobs. We have used that as the driving philosophy for our growth, and we will continue to do so.

Thomas C. Sullivan is chairman and chief executive officer of RPM, Inc. and is responsible for long-term policies and strategies and corporate relations. He took leadership of the *company in 1971. At that time, RPM was a single company known as Republic Powdered Metals, and sales were about $11 million. Today, the company consists of some 40 operating companies and has sales of approximately $2.01 billion.*

RPM has a strong long-term track record with investors that includes 54 consecutive years of record sales, increased earnings for 53 of 54 years, 27 consecutive years of dividend increases, 11 stock dividends since 1976, and an annual compounded rate of return of approximately 18 percent since 1975. Much of this growth is due to the company's acquisition program, which is focused on strong brand names in the building maintenance and protection products fields worldwide.

In addition to RPM, Mr. Sullivan is chairman of the National Paint & Coatings Association and serves on the boards of Pioneer-Standard Electronics, National City Bank, Huffy Corporation, and Kaydon Corporation.

Prior to joining RPM, he served as a communications officer on a battleship in the U.S. Navy. A 1959 graduate of Miami (Ohio) University, Mr. Sullivan earned a Bachelor of Science degree in business administration.

Gaining and Maintaining Entrepreneurial Momentum

Myron P. Shevell

New England Motor Freight

Chairman and Chief Executive Officer

Making a Game Plan

Even the smallest companies need a plan. Being an entrepreneur is a journey, and no one should be on this kind of journey without a road map or set of directions. You can't make any decisions about finances, customers, hiring, or purchasing until you know where you want to take your company. The plan should be written, and you have to keep reviewing and updating it.

I first got involved with New England Motor Freight (NEMF) because the dairy that owned it asked me to come in and look it over. It was doing horribly. It wasn't until about a year later that I decided to buy it.

NEMF wasn't a startup. It had been in business nearly 60 years when I took it over. Still, it was vitally important to have a game plan. This applies to any business – startup or acquisition. You can't shoot from the hip. You need to have a solid idea of where you are and what you want to do.

First I came in and observed what the company was doing so I could find out exactly where it was, both operationally and financially, and what resources it had in terms of staff, equipment and facilities.

Once I did that, I could sit down and make a plan. My first objective was to review the company's current business and analyze it to see what was profitable. I used some very broad rules of thumb to find costs for labor, equipment, insurance, etc. Then I backed those costs into the business they were doing and determined what was profitable and what was not.

Some people make the mistake of going after volume or market share. I've always felt there was no reason to be doing a piece of business unless it was profitable.

In reviewing NEMF's business, we looked at everything, and it was a tremendous help. We located one of the biggest holes in the company when I simply walked out onto our huge dock and saw it was loaded with crude rubber. I asked how much we were getting paid to have the rubber on our dock. I learned we were doing it for nothing, storing it for nothing, unloading the containers for nothing, and then trans-shipping the containers to Massachusetts and coming back empty.

When I sat down with a pencil and paper to calculate it – taking into consideration the warehousing, the space available, the labor, and everything else we weren't getting paid for – we were getting paid $400 a load, and it was costing us about $600 to $700.

My first goal was to make the rubber business profitable or eliminate it. We ceased doing business with the company, and that automatically opened up a whole new area for us. We now had space to work on our dock – space that had been unavailable to us before and was costing us money in addition.

For another customer, we shipped copper rods to New England. When we looked at that business, we found we were losing $200 to $300 a load. We met with the customer about a rate increase and, when they refused, we stopped handling the business.

The important lesson here was not to try to keep business at any cost. This company had been holding onto business that was costing it money with every transaction. It was also tying up resources that probably could have been used for profitable business.

Knowledge = Opportunity

Information is important to any business. Of course, you have to know your own business well. But you also have to know about your customers, your competition, industry trends, the business climate, and innumerable other things. Read a lot. See what the trade press and business press are saying about your industry. Try to follow the economic forecasts; see what conditions are expected to change. Stay close to your industry. Be active in your industry association. Keep up with the various types of equipment that are in development and will be coming online. Do some of this through industry publications, but also meet with manufacturers to learn what they have in the pipeline.

Share your information with your staff, and have them share theirs with you. Everyone has different ways of getting information, and you need to combine and compare and analyze it to have an idea of where things are going. It takes a wide variety of information from many different areas to keep you up on the business.

Some people think they're too busy to do this kind of information-gathering. We spend a lot of time on it. Our business, or any business, is changing all the time. Our customers, the types of business, equipment, regulations, and tax laws may all change. The threat of terrorism in the country has changed the way businesses operate. In some cases, that presents obstacles; in others, opportunities.

We consider it a constant requirement of any senior executive to keep up with every facet of the business – what's changing, what might change, and how those changes might affect us.

Having information isn't enough, though. One of the great entrepreneurial skills is being able to assess that information, relate it to business conditions, and use it to your advantage when the opportunity arises. But first you need to have the information. This is a case where what you don't know will hurt you.

Shortly after I came to NEMF, there was a UPS strike. I knew this would mean a tremendous amount of package volume that normally went through UPS would be directed to the Post Office. From friends in the Post Office, I also knew that they would have difficulty handling the additional volume, and one of the things they would need most was trucks.

The Post Office needed about 1,000 trailers right away, and I was able to immediately acquire 600 trailers. In turn, I leased them to the Post Office. Then we used NEMF tractors to deliver them to various postal installations, and, of course, we generated revenue for doing that. The result was that we were able to put some money in the till, and the company showed a profit for the first time in four years!

Getting on the Right Track

While all this was going on, we were working on the other parts of our game plan. Our analysis showed our labor costs were too high, so we had to lay off the excess people. We cut the staff to the bare minimum. There had been about 20 people in the office, and there were six left afterward. Naturally, there was a lot of agony about letting people go, but the important thing we had to do was get the company's costs under control. If NEMF went bankrupt, everybody would lose their jobs. It's one of the difficult things you have to do sometimes for the long-term good of the company and the people who are left.

At the same time, we replaced some key operations people. This came out of our analysis of our resources – in this case, our staff. We identified some areas where we needed to be stronger and brought in new people.

Because of earlier mismanagement, we also owed a lot of money to suppliers. We couldn't pay them all at once, but we needed them to keep selling to us. I had to find a way to get them the money we owed them while we continued to buy their materials. I met with all of them and told them our new team was in place, and if they would work with us, they would all get paid. Their alternative was to come after us for payment, and we would have to close the company. So they all worked with us, and I kept my word: Every one of them got paid.

After that, we started making the changes we needed so each piece of business – in this case, each truckload of goods – would be profitable. We revised all the routes and changed the value of the freight each truck had to have on it before it could go out. We changed the load factor because we had much more freight going to New England than coming out of

New England. We wanted to make sure, therefore, that we had a heavy load factor going up, since we were running light coming back.

But that was just a temporary fix. The real way to make the business profitable was to increase the amount of freight we were carrying on the return trip. So, simultaneously, I sought customers I knew and had dealt with previously.

One of those customers was a liquor company in Hartford. We began bringing down their products to various distributors in Long Island, New York, and New Jersey. They had no need for immediate service, so they would hold the freight until we had trucks available. At night, instead of having our trucks come down empty all the way from Boston or Providence to New Jersey, they came as far as Hartford and picked up a load of liquor to bring the rest of the way. This was a high-value product, and the revenue we made from bringing liquor from Hartford to New Jersey was as much as we would have made for bringing other kinds of freight from Boston.

In this situation, we had to make sure we kept our eyes on the real goal: to make each run profitable. Balancing outbound and inbound freight is an important principle in the trucking industry, but if we had focused on having full trucks leaving Boston, we would have missed this opportunity. Even though we were running empty for part of the return trip, we were able to accomplish the real goal because of the value of the freight we picked up in Hartford.

Growing Sensibly

Virtually every business wants to grow, but that growth should be planned and controlled and should match the business plan. Recently, a lot of technology companies borrowed and spent incredible amounts of money without paying attention to how much revenue was coming in. As they learned, it was a recipe for disaster.

Once we were in the black and had some business coming in, we were ready to go after more; however, we would need equipment. We didn't yet have the money to buy new equipment. I also didn't want to burden the company with too much debt, since we had just worked so hard to get our heads above water.

I took some of the older equipment and started to repair it. One of my former trailer mechanics agreed to work part-time and put brakes on about a dozen trailers that were sitting on blocks. I took some of the money we had started to make and bought tires. Soon, the trailers were roadworthy.

We also had a number of tractors that didn't run. I sent them to outside repair shops and had them fixed, so we could put them on the road. In the meantime, I got some owner-operators to help us move the freight until we got our own power units running.

That's how we got NEMF off the ground. The most important objective was to get the business profitable. And we did that by re-analyzing all the freight and finding out what was not profitable. In particular, the rubber account and the copper rod account were devastating.

Eliminating those accounts helped us reduce our losses. We were able to take resources the company had been using to lose money and turn them toward profitable business.

Last, but not least important, we remained creative and flexible enough that we were able to take advantage of the Post Office's sudden need for trucks or the opportunity to pick up profitable backhaul loads in Hartford instead of Boston. And, because the company wasn't in the position to spend a lot of money or incur debt, we found ways to make the best use of our limited resources.

From that point, we directed our efforts toward building our company. Because we had gotten our costs under control and were making a profit, and because we were able to work out a deal with our suppliers to get them paid, a year later I was able to go to a bank and borrow $500,000. That gave me some working capital, and we could start to buy some new equipment.

Anticipating Change

As we were getting the company moving, I recognized that trucking deregulation was just around the corner. I tried to look at what that would mean to the industry and our company and to decide what we had to do to be ready and competitive.

What it meant was that the government would no longer control truck routes or rates. Virtually any trucking company would be able to compete for any piece of business. I knew this would spell disaster for companies that were stuck with costs based on a regulated environment. The opportunities would be there for us to expand tremendously beyond what we had been doing until then. I had to start guiding the company for what I thought the future was going to be.

What we needed was a labor agreement we could live with. This was the most important aspect of being ready for the new deregulated world. At the time, labor represented 60 cents of each dollar of our costs.

I met with the union, and with the approval of all the men, froze our seniority list at the level where it was when I came into the company. They also agreed that any additional people we hired would be paid different (lower) rates than the national master contract. We guaranteed the union workers who were with the company at the time that they would receive the benefits that were in the national master contract, but new people would be under a much different bargaining agreement.

As it turned out, I was right. Many companies that were saddled with an outmoded cost structure couldn't make it when deregulation came. The trucking industry has been ravaged by takeovers and bankruptcies over the last 20 years. Many of the oldest and most respected names in the industry have disappeared.

At NEMF, because we had our costs under control, we were ready for the new, more competitive environment. We capitalized on the opportunities deregulation presented, and we've been fortunate to enjoy tremendous growth in that same period.

Teamwork

It almost goes without saying that people have to work together for a business to succeed. Building an effective team starts with getting good people. But members of the team should examine and object and criticize things as part of the decision-making process. What goes with that, however, is to then develop solutions – better ways of doing things.

To have a good team, everyone has to feel he or she has a voice and is heard. Disagreement should never come out of a personal agenda or for the sake of being disruptive. People shouldn't take criticism personally, and everyone should be focused on what's best for the company. The objective is to make the company perform better for the customer, be more profitable, become a better place to work.

That takes a cohesive group. They don't have to agree with each other all the time, but everyone has to recognize that when the group makes a decision, then they all pull in the same direction.

There has to be a leader, too. If the team gets off-course, then it's up to the leader to steer it back in line. If the leader promotes his ideas first, the members of the team will tend to go along. Eventually they will stop contributing their own input. If the leader acts as more of a guide, letting the group work out solutions, but keeping them on track, the team will be more self-motivated and dynamic. More and better ideas will emerge.

Dealing with a Turbulent Economy

After all these years in the trucking business, I've lived through plenty of economic ups and downs. If you want to know which way the economy is headed, talk to a trucker. We always feel the impact of changing economic conditions first.

Never forget there is a business cycle. There will be good times; there will be bad times. Neither will last forever.

The best way to manage for a bad economy is to manage properly when times are good. That means being prepared for the inevitable downturn in the economy. Don't spend every dollar you make. Put some in reserve, and operate your business on a conservative basis. This sounds like common sense, but you'd be surprised at how many businesses fail because people ignored that principle. If you do that, when you come to a turbulent time, you'll have the resources to ride out the storm.

First, make sure you're not over-leveraged. That's why we didn't start borrowing money as soon as we got into the black. If you're over-leveraged when the economy turns bad, no matter what you do, it will have serious adverse effects – maybe even permanent effects – and you may not be able to come out of it.

Know your actual costs and your break-even point. Price pressure usually becomes a very important factor in a bad economy. If you're managing your business properly and have to cut prices to retain your top-line volume, making little or no money for a while, you're able to do that to get through the storm. But if you don't have the flexibility of that kind of cushion, then you can't ride it out. If a recession lasts for an extended period of time – say, two or three years – then it can wipe you out.

I've always looked at our business not in terms of how much we can make, but how much we can lose. That's at least in part based on my failure in my younger days. If you think of your business that way, you'll manage so that nothing that can happen is ever so bad it can cripple your company. The most that can happen is that you may miss some opportunities in business. But if you overextend yourself, it can destroy your company.

Controlling costs during turbulent times is very important. But again, this is a great habit to form when times are good. If you're a free spender in good times, you may not be able to grab the reins quickly enough when the economy spirals down.

An often overlooked factor in dealing with a turbulent economy is the internal environment. It's most important to keep the morale of your people up during that period.

Employee morale needs to remain high on an ongoing basis. If you ignore your employees in boom times and start trying to build morale when things get rough, they'll see right through you.

Delivering the Goods

The expression "delivering the goods" comes from the trucking industry, of course. But every business has to deliver the goods in the sense of getting its product or service to the customer and making sure that customer is satisfied. Making sure your company is executing at every level is essential in any business.

I recommend setting goals for every area of the company and rewarding people for excellence. Naturally, your rewards program should be tailored to your company and your industry.

Our company, for example, has different kinds of rewards, depending on the function. There is an incentive program for operations people. Sales people, of course, are rewarded through their revenues. Senior managers are rewarded according to how well their areas of responsibility perform. We reward our maintenance people according to how well they maintain the equipment. We also recognize outstanding team performance. We have a monthly program to honor the best-performing terminals.

We've developed what we call our "Chain of Quality." It breaks down every shipment into a series of transactions. Responsibility for each "link" in the chain is assigned to a worker. We conduct continual training of production and clerical workers on their responsibilities in the chain. The chain forms a circle, beginning and ending with the customer.

We measure performance for each link against specific performance-based criteria. We set goals for each facet and then reward people for exceeding those goals. We can see how well we're doing by measuring our performance against the goals. Each year, we raise the bar, so we're constantly improving. That's how it's been since my first days with NEMF – a constant program of trying to do things better.

"Selling" Your Company

Every business needs to get its message across to its clients or customers. How you "sell" yourself is the first step in building a long-term, trusting relationship with a client.

I believe this "selling" works best when the client knows exactly who you are and what you're good at. We don't oversell to our customers. This goes back to making sure to seek only prof able bі siness. If we tried to do something for a customer thaі isn't iіı our part of the market, we could wind up losing money and having an unhappy customer. That customer won't be back when he really needs our services.

We have a select clientele whose shipping needs we can meet very well, and we operate our business with them in mind. We can't be everything to everybody. So we focus on the different niches of the business that our company does well – our overnight service, our guaranteed service, and our customized and personalized service that goes with our being one of the last of the major family-owned trucking companies.

Those are our strengths, and we sell them: If you're a customer, you're important to us; you're not just another number on a sheet. You have the luxury of having the owners of the company right there all the time, watching out for your business, knowing that we're just an extension to your customers.

It's just as important that you "sell" your company internally. The techniques we use for our customers hold for our workers. (We prefer "workers" to "employees.") We treat them like individuals and let them know they are not just another number in one of these large trucking conglomerates. We care for each of them personally.

One example of how we do this is our Worker Appreciation Week, an annual event in which at least one of the top five senior managers comes to each of 30 terminals for a breakfast or a dinner, shakes every worker's hand, and presents each one with a gift.

Of course, throughout the year, we all continue to visit our facilities to talk to our people and let them know they're part of a family. We try to create an environment where their work is done on a personal basis, rather than a functional one. They feel personally responsible for the growth and building of the company. We allow our people a lot of flexibility. We attract a lot of top people because they want to work in that kind of climate, rather than be a small cog in a huge corporation.

I also think it's important that we sell our company in the political arena. So I have served as chairman of the New Jersey Motor Truck Association and as vice chairman of NJ Transit, the state commuter transportation agency. That has helped us become a leader and a respected part of the larger community. It also gives us the ear of government leaders, so we can help them recognize the importance of transportation.

We try to make our workers aware that we are always selling ourselves to the public in general. We pay attention to the way our equipment looks on the road, the way our drivers respect the highways. Trucks aren't small. They are very visible, and people recognize our equipment on the road. That gives us another dimension in the public's eye. It may not matter in terms of direct access to business, but it helps people form an impression of the company. If it's a good one, you never know who is out there to have that impression made. Every public contact is a chance for the company to be better known and respected in the business world.

Not every company has its name rolling down the highway on a 53-foot trailer. But we all encounter the public in some way, even if it's just answering the phone. It's important to make the most of those brief contacts with the public and leave them with a positive view of our company.

Serving the Customer

One of the main ideas we try to convey to everyone at New England Motor Freight is that "The customer is King (or Queen)." If you don't service the customer – give him what you assured him would – you're not going to be in business.

You stay in business by selling what you can deliver, but not trying to be all things to all people. If you oversell and can't deliver, that's worse than almost anything else you can do in business.

Set your service standards; live by those standards; and give your customer that and a little extra – a pleasant voice on the phone, a happy driver on the dock, a nice piece of equipment pulling up to the building. If you give that kind of customer service at a rate that's reasonable for the customer, but that allows you to continue to buy equipment, hire the best people, have the best technology, and make a legitimate profit, your customers will be happy, and your business will succeed. All this depends on what kind of customer service you provide.

This takes time. It doesn't happen overnight. It starts with the head of the company and works its way on down. Leading by example is crucial. What you expect from your people is what you get. If they know you are just as devoted and involved as they are in getting the job done, then you'll get it done as a team. You have to get everyone in the company to buy in and acknowledge that there is no business without the customer. If you take care of the customer, your business will be taken care of. If you made a promise to the customer, you'd better fulfill it.

This rule applies throughout business and is especially true in our industry, because a piece of freight goes through a tremendous number of different hands to arrive intact and on time. It's not only the person who has direct contact with the customer who gives customer service. If the dockman decided to load the freight in the wrong trailer, or the mechanic didn't do the job to get the truck on the road, then the freight doesn't get there on time.

All the people who are part of this entire sequence constitute the real customer service, even though the customer never sees most of them. Everyone has to understand that in the chain of quality, if anyone doesn't do his or her job, it can destroy customer service.

Entrepreneurial Momentum

Momentum, like many other aspects of an entrepreneurial business, starts from the top. The entrepreneur has to come to work every day and provide the spark, the inspiration, the creativity, and the leadership that drive the company forward. It's hard to imagine how anyone can do that if he or she doesn't feel passionate about the work.

I've been around trucks for as long as I can remember, and I've always loved them. I knew at a very early age what business I wanted to go into. In 22 years, the Shevell Group of businesses, including New England Motor Freight, Inc., Eastern Freight Ways, Inc., and Carrier Industries, has grown to an organization with 3,500 employees and 4,000 tractors and trailers, with annual revenues approaching $300 million.

You have to love what you do and love the people around you. If you do, you will not settle for mediocrity. You'll always want to push for excellence. Having those values will lead to success.

Myron P. (Mike) Shevell is chairman and CEO of New England Motor Freight, Inc. He is responsible for the overall strategic direction of the company. He is also chairman of the Shevell Group of real estate, trucking, and logistics companies, which includes Carrier Industries, Eastern Freight Ways, Apex Logistics, NEMF World Transport, and NEMF of Canada.

Under his leadership, the company has grown from 55 units and five terminals to more than 6,000 pieces of equipment and 30 terminals throughout the Northeast and is now the region's fastest-growing family-owned LTL carrier. NEMF also boasts terminals in Florida, Puerto Rico, and Canada and reaches 80 percent of the U.S. population through service partnerships.

Mr. Shevell was named 1999 Master Entrepreneur in the Ernst & Young Entrepreneur of the Year Awards. The Master Entrepreneur designation recognizes an individual who has maintained management excellence over a sustained period of time. It is one of the most prestigious awards that can be given to an independent business owner in the United States. In March of 2000, he was presented the Salzberg Medallion for Transportation by Syracuse University. It is one of the most highly regarded awards in the transportation field.

Mr. Shevell received an associate degree from George Washington University and a bachelor's degree from New York University. He also attended the Academy of Advanced Traffic.

Mr. Shevell is chairman of the New Jersey Motor Truck Association and vice chairman of the board of directors of New Jersey Transit. He is a regional director of the Bank of New York, N.A. He is also a member of the National Defense Executive Reserve of the U.S. Department of Transportation, the Traffic Club of North Jersey, and the Raritan Traffic Club.

Creating a Culture that Ensures Success

Justin Jaschke

Verio

Chief Executive Officer

Management Style Makes a Difference

My management style emphasizes a perfect fit – that is, ensuring that the right people with the best skills are in the right positions. If there is one area critical to an executive's success, it is recruiting, motivating, and retaining talented people. In addition, I take a broad view of things and focus on the end game, the goals and objectives that this team of people is trying to achieve. I want to ensure alignment between where the company is heading and those key people in supporting roles to help achieve overall corporate goals. I employ an inquisitive style with my team to ensure they are on track with their work, and projects are being completed. I tend to ask questions continually, until the issues are resolved or the answers clearly address ongoing situations.

I am also a big believer in providing the right environment for success. One important element a leader needs when building a successful company is creating a culture that will enable you to succeed. There are various kinds of organizational cultures, all of which can be successful. The military has a command-and-control culture, which works well in that environment. Some companies have a nurturing culture, where people get a great deal of help and support; school environments are probably more typical of that. I would characterize the culture I have built as competency-based, typified by people who are very good at what they do, who are self-directed and flexible in their approach to their jobs. In this environment people are expected to deliver outcomes based on their competency and ability to accomplish agreed upon goals – in essence, a culture based on results and performance.

I think ours is a very driven environment, where people work hard, are very enthusiastic about what they do, and enjoy their work. I have been accused of being the work-hard, play-hard type, and that gets reflected in the culture to some extent, where there is a lot of focus and energy on getting things done, but people have fun along the way.

Of course, all of this depends on your ability to communicate your vision. You have to find multiple ways to do this, and what I have found, time and time throughout my career, is that you cannot over-communicate. The adage in education that you have to repeat something six times before it can be retained is true in business, as well.

As a leader, to be convincing to your employees, you must be convinced about the vision you're laying out. You have to simplify the communication of this vision down to a set of strong statements and visuals that clearly communicate it. Finally, you have to commit to talking about it in a variety of forums, using different formats.

At Verio, we conduct road-show presentations, traveling to various offices, getting in front of multiple associate groups, and explaining firsthand what we're trying to do and the basic strategy that will help the company meet its goals. We also do town-hall meetings where we can address employee questions, follow up with written communiqués that provide associates with the state of the organization, and take the opportunity to explain the direction of the company and the vision in yet another format. We recently assembled a video that was sent to all our locations that communicated the same message, again reinforcing our commitment to the message and repeating it in an interesting way. Using a multimedia tool as basic as a video presentation, we were able to use another touch point to communicate to our associates.

My advice to other leaders is, whenever possible, find different avenues to communicate to your associates and your leadership team in meaningful ways. Even with this outreach, you will sometimes be faced with employees who don't fully understand your message, especially in an environment where the strategy, and thus the communications about it, changes often. This is all the more reason to communicate more consistently and more frequently.

In addition, your senior team should get on board and personally take responsibility to effectively and consistently communicate your company's strategy and vision. To do this and to help ensure success, use every opportunity with your senior leadership team to once again reiterate the vision. This not only helps ensure they can recite it in their sleep, but more importantly that this team is fully invested in the company's vision and how it translates into success. This investment is crucial, as key leaders then communicate that vision throughout the rest of the organization. The so-called task of "reading off the same sheet of music" is certainly helpful, but more importantly, the notes should result in a grand melody.

Striving for Individual Success

When I am hiring staff, I look for smart people with a strong track record of success. I have a very intuitive approach to selecting people; many times I cannot explain specifically why I'm prepared to hire the individual. During the hiring process, I look for a connection between the individual and myself. I look for people who are enthusiastic, energetic, and optimistic, and then I try to match their skills to specific job requirements. I go back to the old NFL recruiting philosophy initially espoused by the Dallas Cowboys: Look for the best available athlete, not necessarily the person with some specific skill. I would rather hire someone who has very good raw talent and could be brought up to speed on the needs of the position. I try to find the person with the best overall talent, who is the smartest, brightest, most enthusiastic individual.

In my experience, you get the most out of your employees by providing them with freedom to do what they do best, enabling them to be creative and to try new things, and most importantly, listening to them. Employees who have a desire to make an impact and to do an even better job should have the opportunity to excel.

There are however, a few key elements to this: You have to provide them with the data and the context so they can understand the circumstances. Also, you need to paint the vision and get them believing in it, to have them feel compelled by it so they understand where you are trying to go. Finally, you need to give them the freedom and the flexibility to approach the job in the way they think is best. There is always more than one way to tackle a specific job, and I think that early in my career I was more concerned with having people do it my way; then I learned through experience that you are a better leader when you allow people to make their own choices so as to create their own method that allows them to succeed and reach overall goals. It has become apparent that people tend to be more effective leveraging their own style and capabilities as they see best to get the job done. So paint the vision; make sure they understand the objectives; give them the data and the information to evaluate the circumstances and understand the business; and allow them the freedom to approach their job the way they think they can be most effective.

The Power of Persuasion

To become a leader you need to have a firm grasp of the business, a framework for how the business fits together; and you must know the pieces that will make it successful. This provides organizational context for how you are trying to manage that business. A good leader has a grasp of what is possible and the ability to formulate a vision. You also need optimism that you can achieve your goals in spite of all odds. Some people say that to continue against long odds is unrealistic, but I believe a leader needs to be confident and optimistic to overcome the odds. As a leader, you must believe it can be done and must be convincing enough to get people to follow you.

That is another requirement of leadership – you have to be convincing. You have to be able to persuade people to follow you. You have to be a salesperson at heart. You may not be front-line selling a product, but you are certainly selling the vision and the opportunity. What impresses me most in other leaders is the ability to encapsulate a vision and make it compelling. One of the people I most admire is John F. Kennedy: He was able to convey a vision through his words, and he got people excited and enthusiastic about that vision.

Most successful leaders must have a strong element of persuasion to motivate and convince people they should follow. In addition, you need a high tolerance for responsibility – you have to like it, in fact. You have to be the one who will make the final call when data and advice fall on both sides, and you must be prepared to take the blame when things don't go as planned.

Managing in Turbulent Times

I tend to gravitate toward a growing and building type of environment. I am by nature very much an optimist, so I typically don't feel constrained or pulled back, or attempt to manage against the downside. Rather, I work aggressively to build for the upside. My approach in a turbulent environment tends to be one that ensures I have people who are good at managing the downside, and I give them the freedom to make the choices necessary to stay aligned with the overall vision. It's not that I am unrealistic, but I certainly tend to lean toward the optimistic side, and it is hard for me to focus too much on the negative.

To me, that is an important trait in leadership – people look to others who are optimistic about the future, and they are more compelled to follow that lead. In a downside environment, you have to mute that message to some extent and let the choice to take risks drive the trade-offs you must make to succeed in a turbulent environment. I would characterize this current environment as being similar to a desert. Capital has dried up; we are in drought conditions;

and there are fires burning down companies. You have to focus on identifying the elements of your company that can survive a desert environment with the least amount of capital and the least amount of water. That is tougher for me to do when I am so enthusiastic about the future and see the possibilities down the road. You have to have people around you who can balance that thinking during these times.

My opinion is that it is possible to make money in any environment, depending on the business. I think the trade-off is between growth and profitability.

In good times, when things are thriving, that trade-off tends to swing toward the growth side. In down times, you have to sacrifice much more in terms of future growth and what you are investing to control cash burn and profitability in the near term. Even for us, elements of our business are profitable in this environment that we focus more heavily on, and the things that require more investment and more capital to grow tend to get starved in this situation. So you naturally sacrifice some growth, with the assumption that when things recover you can revitalize the investment in those areas of the business and capitalize on the growth. This kind of balancing challenges management; it's why executives are empowered to make those decisions.

My view is that the only sustainable business advantage these days is the ability to learn faster than your competitors. I try to capitalize on change by continuing to learn about the business and keeping an open mind to change and how you can take advantage of it. We go through a set of strategic planning exercises every six months, and part of that strategic planning session is to look at our competitive landscape and understand our competitors' strengths, and then do what we call smart-bombing exercises. If X is your competitor, what can you do to differentiate yourself from them and take advantage of gaining business? Then flip it around and ask: What can the same competitor do to gain more business by capitalizing on your weaknesses?

It is essential to be knowledgeable about the environment and to understand the core changes in technology, in purchasing patterns, and in the way you are doing business that could lead to a disruptive change. You then need to set a strategy that allows you to eliminate the disadvantages and capitalize on the advantages to position yourself in front of the wave of change. Most successful venture businesses are built on identifying a wave of change that is hitting across an industry – the development of wireless technologies, for example. That was a big change that was obviously going to affect the way people communicate. The ability to get in front of that wave and create a business that would ride on that wave of change was critical. The Internet was another big wave of change, not only for how people communicate, but increasingly how companies conduct business. Positioning a business plan to be able to get in front of that wave of change and capture the growth was critical. Now we are going through yet another wave of change that is partly based on a change in assumptions about economic growth, and partly related to a change in attitudes towards security and redundancy that has implications for what we need to be focused on in our own company. It is important to understand that and get in front of it to manage through those alterations and capitalize on them.

I do a lot of scanning to stay abreast of change. We also have an internal group that does industry scanning and sends out regular e-mails about key articles and news items to keep the leadership teams abreast of changes. In addition, I get a number of periodicals. I first review the table of contents so I can scan for interest, and then choose to read those articles that appeal to me. I always carry a stack of reading material in my briefcase, so when I'm on a plane or in the dentist's office, I can pull an article out and read it for relevant information. I think success comes from having a healthy appetite for learning. I was always a good student and loved to learn, and I think that is something you have to continue throughout life.

Building a Hundred-Year Company

Building a company that will last a hundred years is a matter of going through the various phases and taking the appropriate steps in each one. In the early phases you are just trying to survive and initiate something that can grow. Then it is a matter of staying on top of it, growing it, and fueling it with the right amount of capital and people. Eventually it becomes a matter of institutionalizing it – the phase we are in now. In the early days of building the company you are much more dependent on heroic acts of individuals to get there. As the company matures and grows, you have to move away from dependence on these acts to the dependence on solid process and business discipline. You have to instill the kinds of long-term, sustainable processes that can be continued as people inevitably move in and out of the business and the company. It is a matter of having the right plans in place, both from a personnel standpoint and a business standpoint – understanding what is changing your environment and reacting to that. From a capital standpoint, you may realize you need to become part of a bigger entity to survive.

One thing that strikes me, having been through different companies, is that they are amazingly resilient entities. It is actually pretty hard to kill a business once you get it to a certain size and scale. I have seen businesses go through enormous turmoil and change and still survive situations you would have never thought they could withstand. Part of that is getting it to a certain critical mass and scale and getting processes and business practices in place that can allow a company's survival even as people change and the business evolves.

A key element in building a lasting company is managing risk. One way we have always approached risk management is to have multiple options. We have always tried to work multiple paths so we are not held captive to one solution or have only one alternative. Throughout our acquisition history, we have typically negotiated two or three potential acquisitions at once, so we were not forced to take on an acquisition at a price we did not find attractive, or we weren't left empty-handed. This has been the same practice as with partnerships. If you need a certain type of relationship to be successful, you want to pursue multiple paths simultaneously to get there. You deal with risk around choices you have to make. We try to do financial modeling and try to understand upsides and downsides, and understand the balance in the decision we are making.

Another way you manage risk is by contingency planning. If things go wrong – and they can't always be perfect – you need to have a backup plan. The other important thing is to have a healthy debate and variety of views. As mentioned before, my views tend to lean toward the optimistic side, and it is healthy to have more conservative and somewhat skeptical views on the table so we can consider all perspectives before making a decision.

Ultimately, there are three rules to building a company that will last. The paramount rule is don't run out of money. That is a piece of advice I first received when I decided to leave the consulting business early in my career and start my own business. The senior consulting partner sat me down when I was heading out the door and said, "I hate to lose you at this point, but as long as you are convinced you are going to go, the only advice I can offer is that once you start a business, it is a race against cash flow. You have to get the cash flow positive before you run out of money, and if you don't, the consequences are severe." That has been echoed throughout my venture capital experience, where as soon as you complete one financing, you're into another to try to raise capital. You see it in this market where you have an industry just littered with the bodies of companies that have run out of money. Many of them had good business plans, and even good execution; but a lot of them just got extended too far and were not ready for the downturn. So rule number one is don't run out of money.

The second rule is remember the importance of people. My own belief is that people are the most critical element, and it was probably best put by my former chairman, who liked to say, "Nothing is impossible, as long as you don't have to do it yourself."

There is a third rule, which is a risk-management kind of mantra: "Run the business as if you are going to own it forever, or you probably will." You may eventually sell the company, but you should think as though none of those other things will happen. When you are running it as if you will own it forever, and the business is healthy and thriving, then a lot of other options, like potential acquirers, or strategic partners, open up to you. But if you are assuming, even relying on, those other avenues, you can find yourself in a real trap.

Measuring Success

There is a broad set of metrics that are used to measure success. The first and foremost for an entrepreneur is the stock value. Earlier in our development, our success was measured by our ability to get capital to fund the business. That is a very tangible measure of support for what you are doing, which depends on your ability to show a track record of financial performance in terms of revenue growth and development. Then, once you go public, you track the stock price, which is again driven by communicating success on the operational side and from the financial metrics that show the key strategic initiatives indicating that the company is improving its position. Our current environment, where we are a subsidiary of NTT Communications Corporation, is much more driven by those financial metrics, where we are looking at revenue growth, profitability, and improvement in cost structure. But still, we have developed a phantom stock-option tracking mechanism that allows us to track something comparable to a public stock price. This will continue to be one measure of success over time as we try to drive that up.

Then there are strategic positioning elements – our ability to strike key relationships, to put key capabilities in place, and to develop and get new products out the door. Ultimately, you try to develop a key set of metrics. Then in the strategic planning exercises, we set goals for metrics, such as revenue growth, specific revenue by product, cost metrics, profit metrics, or others, such as intent to complete certain acquisitions, intent to have certain key relationships in place, and intent to get specific products out the door.

Another important measure of success is your ability to attract and retain talent. That is an indication of your success in building an organization that people want to be associated with and that has some longevity.

A final way is public perception – what is being said about the company, how it is viewed by customers and other external constituencies.

The Future of Management

As far as I can tell, the requirement to learn and adapt at an ever-increasing pace only continues to intensify. In that kind of environment, management will become less one-person-centric and more team-oriented. Because things move so fast and because there is so much information to grasp, the ability for one person to do it all becomes more and more challenging, and you will have to rely on a team. You will still have one person in the CEO position, but I think the burdens of that position will be spread more evenly across a broader management team to deal with the complexity and speed of change.

I think that leading in the new economy will depend less on physical presence and more on virtual kinds of companies, and leaders will have to learn to be comfortable with a much broader array of communication vehicles – e-mail, teleconferencing, telephones, as well as in person – because of the virtual nature of management.

I also think management will take an increasingly global perspective. The major trend in the world today is globalization – the breakdown of technological, capital, and market barriers, and the sharing of technology, capital, and knowledge across geographic boundaries. You'll therefore have to be much more comfortable dealing with diversity, dealing with different cultural nuances across the various parts of your company, and incorporating a broader range of management styles and approaches to be able to deal with globalization.

Justin L. Jaschke has served as chief executive officer and a director of Verio since the company's inception in March 1996. Before forming Verio, Mr. Jaschke served as chief operating officer for Nextel Communications Inc., following its merger with OneComm Corp. in July 1995. Mr. Jaschke served as OneComm's president and as a member of its board of directors from the time he joined that company in April 1993 until the company's merger with Nextel.

From May 1990 to April 1993, Mr. Jaschke served as president and chief executive officer of Bay Area Cellular Telephone Co. From November 1987 to May 1990, he was vice president of corporate development of PacTel Cellular, and from 1985 to 1987, he was director of mergers and acquisitions for PacTel Corp. Prior to that, Mr. Jaschke was a management consultant with Marakon Associates.

Mr. Jaschke currently serves on the board of directors of Dobson Communications, a rural cellular and local exchange provider; the board of directors of Agilera, a full-service application service provider (ASP); and on the Puget Sound Board of Trustees.

Mr. Jaschke received a Bachelor of Science degree summa cum laude in mathematics from the University of Puget Sound and a Master of Science degree in management from the Sloan School of Management at MIT.

Maintaining Traditional Values in a Culture of Constant Change

Richard B. Priory

Duke Energy
Chairman of the Board, President, Chief Executive Officer

The Steady Pulse of Change

In today's business world, receptivity to change is a key imperative. The leaders in our company must possess both a mindset and a skill set that enable them to anticipate and master change. Too often in the past, business professionals have viewed the ability to deal with change as a "coping" response. You weathered or endured change but certainly didn't invite it into your company or business environment! The healthier viewpoint, in my opinion, is to open the window wide and let the winds of change stir things up. Change is accelerating; it's transforming; and it's affecting every market we serve, every region on our map, every service we offer, and every one of us.

Change is an empowering force that has allowed my company and many others to grow in positive new directions. Over the past decade, the energy industry has evolved dramatically. Electric restructuring in the U.S., privatization of international markets, the convergence of gas and power, and new technologies have all profoundly redefined our industry and outlook for the future. Those changes have been hard for some organizations to grapple with, and as a result, we've seen our competitive field narrow as the strong and agile prevailed over the more narrowly focused. True to Darwin's theory, natural selection occurs in business, as well as in nature. We've been fortunate in that we have a strong foundation and an ability to adapt quickly to changing environmental conditions.

I enjoy the constant pulse of change and the challenges and rich opportunities it brings. And I tend to surround myself with individuals who are likewise inspired and energized by the changing dimensions of our business environment. Our world is a complex kaleidoscope of shifting parts. Depending on your perspective, you see either advantage or chaos, opportunity or threat. And how you approach the lens is key to competitive success.

Change can be daunting at first, especially given the magnitude and pace that confronts us today. But business leaders need to become accomplished at managing the diversity of issues, problems, and challenges that come in the door. The leaders in Duke Energy must be able to manage change as adeptly as they manage people, projects, and financial results.

Ours is a competitive business, but competition, like change, is healthy. I enjoy competition and always have. From Little League to the board room and the golf course, I've found competition to be motivating, rewarding, and, at times, humbling. We tend to win our fair share, and we lose some, as well, to worthy competitors. But both wins and losses should motivate your team – to either continue the streak or turn the tide. The win/loss cycle keeps you balanced. You pause – briefly! – to celebrate accomplishments and focus on the need to do better the next time around. Just when you think you have the competitive advantage, a good player comes along and knocks you down a peg or two. In the long view, those strong players who bring something new to the game do us a favor. Their performance makes us realize we have to get better – fast – and reclaim our competitive edge. Our company is full of competitive folks who welcome the chance to test themselves and our strategy against the best, because they realize going head-to-head with strong competitors ultimately makes us better and stronger.

Managing During Turbulent Times

If a business is healthy, growing, and keeping pace with the marketplace and customer needs, then it is by definition turbulent and changing. Turbulence is a transformational force that churns the water and introduces new ideas and approaches.

In business, you're confronted with a constantly changing set of variables – economic conditions, market cycles, technology shifts, regulatory and policy issues, talent and staffing needs – the list goes on. Those variables propel you into a turbulent and somewhat chaotic management of events. Nothing happens the way you expect it will, no matter how well you've planned and prepared. The next day, the event you planned around happens very differently. You come to work in the morning, and an industry crisis arises; oil prices rise or fall dramatically; or a key employee announces he or she has to leave the company for a period of time. You have to work around those variables, without blocking or digressing from your end-objective path.

At Duke Energy, we've learned to take the changes and curveballs in stride. Even a turbulent economy is simply another variable to us. We just throw it into the mix, review our strategy relative to the behavior of the economy, and figure out how we can deliver uninterrupted levels of value and growth to our shareholders. Our entire strategy is designed with the belief that we will see economic activity moving up and down, and that energy commodities are extremely volatile. So we focus on managing change, risk, and market cycles in ways that create value from the inevitable turbulence of our business environment.

Our natural gas gathering and processing business is a good example of managing through up and down cycles. When commodity prices are high, the business makes very few acquisitions because the price of acquisitions gets higher as the commodity price stays up. We'll simply focus on creating a more efficient operation, reducing non-performing assets, and high-grading the assets that are performing well by making key modifications to them. Then as the price of oil drops, the business will focus on acquisitions and growth. We have a business strategy that recognizes turbulence in the marketplace, and we are able to execute and create sustainable value in a variety of scenarios – in gas gathering and in all our businesses.

Positioning the Company Strategically

In 1996, when we created Duke Energy by merging the talent, market expertise, and assets of Duke Power Company and PanEnergy, we crafted a strategy that has withstood the test of time remarkably well. We have modified the plan to keep pace with changing economic and market fundamentals, but our plan remains true to the compass direction we set back in 1996.

That strategy reflects major market and competitive trends: a focus on the high-growth, unregulated businesses that will increasingly contribute to earnings; a fluid portfolio of energy assets and positions; an increased emphasis on trading and marketing and hedging strategies; delivering solutions to today's toughest energy challenges; and the ability to integrate and connect within our enterprise and with our customers and markets.

At Duke Energy, strategic planning is a continuous, collaborative team process that involves all parts of our enterprise. It is truly a cycle in that we develop a long-term view of the world, set enterprise and business unit strategies to succeed in that world, and establish enterprise challenges and specific objectives to implement the strategies. Then, on at least an annual basis, we re-examine our world outlook, refine our strategies, and set new objectives as our world continues to change and as competitive markets continue to evolve.

Our detailed planning activity, which includes forecasts, budgets, capital expenditures, and earnings goals, focuses on both near- and long-term horizons and identifies key signposts that might signal market and economic shifts.

Our charge is to maintain corporate flexibility and willingness to change tactics in mid-stride so we can react faster to competitive changes. Rate of reaction is a point I'd like to emphasize here. Planning should never, ever slow you down. In fact, it should enhance your ability to anticipate and respond. A lot has changed in our world and in our markets. We know the strong operational performance of Duke Energy's predecessor companies isn't enough by itself anymore. We can no longer shape our destiny by just being the best in our respective fields. We also must be the first, the fastest, the most flexible. We must maintain keen market knowledge and insights and be able to seize opportunities, manage risk, and adapt to changes in real time.

Crossing the Bridge Between Planning and Results

Many people can craft elegant and lofty plans. But hammering out a growth strategy – translating directional words into actionable, tangible results – requires top-notch leadership and unparalleled ability to execute. Execution is the toughest part of the equation, but, in my mind, it is also the most defining and rewarding.

If planning is truly strategic, it involves spanning the expanse between where an organization is today and the shared vision of where it will be in the future. The strategic plan is a bridge between two points, one known and one anticipated. It links present state with future state and provides a platform from which a company moves forward.

Forward movement is a key point here because it is easy for an organization that has labored long and hard on a carefully crafted plan to stand forever at bridge portal, admiring its design. We can become very enamored with our plans and the planning process, to the point that we lose sight of the destination.

Ultimately, you have to cross the bridge. You have to take the necessary leap of faith, believing strongly in both the validity of your plan and the vision of your future.

Having an idea is one thing. Getting that idea accomplished is another. In the words of Thomas Edison, "I have more respect for the fellow with a single idea who gets there than for a fellow with a thousand ideas who does nothing."

I constantly focus our team on driving and delivering results – real, quantifiable results. And I caution against declaring victory before we have fully executed our plan and achieved the outcome we sought. A natural human tendency is to coast a bit when the finish line is within view. But that sense of certainty and complacency can be dangerous. We don't count any eggs until the chickens are walking around.

Organizations must gain consensus and clarity about strategic objectives. You do that by communicating – continuously – your strategic objectives to business units, departments, teams, and individuals.

At Duke Energy, we expect every employee to be a strategist, to be able to make the link between his or her specific role and the attainment of our enterprise goals. That's critical to our success.

And if every employee is to be a strategist, the strategy must be clear, widely communicated, and practical and applicable to everyone's job. Employees must have the tools and abilities to make it happen. Duke Energy has a series of enterprise challenges associated with our strategic plan. One of those challenges, strengthening our team, is focused on ensuring our team has the strategic skills, understanding, and ability to move us forward. .

Enterprise Athletes: Empowering Victory

Duke Energy's success is driven by the minds and talent and creativity of our team. Strategy doesn't come together, and results don't materialize, without the accord and resolve of the men and women of Duke Energy. We therefore devote great time and energy to articulating and rolling out, at every level within the company, our strategic plan. Our leadership team is charged with educating their teams about corporate and business unit goals, and with setting clear expectations related to anticipated results. They also help define the very direct role that groups and individuals play in our overall business success. The leaders within Duke Energy carry the strategy torch throughout our organization and make sure everyone is sharply focused on our goals and game plan going forward.

Assigning responsibility is key to execution. We strive to challenge employees to step up to the plate, leave their comfort zones, and grow in new areas. We can point to a number of success stories in which we've moved folks from the regulated side of our company to our competitive businesses, and they have thrived and helped our business thrive. Cross-pollination is important to us.

I like to use the term "enterprise athlete" to describe the model of strength and flexibility we expect of our leaders. A number of key traits define the enterprise athlete.

First of all, the enterprise athlete is able to deliver on commitments. This is a basic, and one I see as critical to all levels and roles in the organization. The ability to execute strategy, to serve customers well with bold solutions and real results, is at the heart of our brand and our reputation. It is foundational in that it reflects on corporate character, as well as corporate performance. Those who know us, those whom we serve, expect us to deliver. I expect us to deliver, and we should all expect that of ourselves and of one another.

From where I sit, I know I have to deliver the numbers to Wall Street. I also know I can't do that alone. I rely on our entire team to deliver on their commitments. For Duke Energy to hit the bold targets we've set, everyone in the company must produce results that roll up and influence business group and corporate results.

Another key expectation I have is that we will respect and value all of those results and contributions. No one business unit, no single person, makes Duke Energy great. We owe our success to our ability to marshal – for the benefit of customers – diverse resources, disciplines, and experience.

Second, leadership courage will be critical going forward. Our competitive position depends on our ability to move with speed, confidence, and courage. We have to be willing to take risks – reasoned risks – and make the tough calls.

We need leaders who can transcend our regulated background, in which caution, deliberation, and precision prevailed. We need leaders who are willing to work outside their comfort zones to bring home the rewards that come with smart risk-taking.

The third attribute I want to mention is leadership maturity. I'm not referring to age or seniority, but to breadth of experience and informed judgment. We need men and women who can make sound, well-thought-out decisions, who are accountable for those decisions and will see them through, and who bring big-picture thinking and big results to our customers and our company.

Someone once said, "Maturity of mind is the capacity to endure uncertainty." We face uncertainty every day; it is the only constant in today's business world. Although we have enormous amounts of data at our fingertips, making predictions about the world in which we will compete is increasingly challenging. Technology, markets, customer expectations, economic indicators, and pricing factors change constantly. The rapid-fire pace of innovation means we'll have tools at our disposal or new pressures at our door that we can't anticipate today.

The leaders of Duke Energy will be those individuals who manage change and exploit opportunities with wisdom, level-headedness, and flexibility.

And finally, we need to integrate and keep good company. I continually emphasize the importance of integration to our company's success. We need to share knowledge, experience, skills, and people across business unit lines. The true leaders of Duke Energy will see and understand beyond their corners of the company. They will have an expansive knowledge of our multi-faceted business. They will cultivate skills that are transferable across business-unit lines. They will volunteer for assignments that offer opportunity for growth and new learning.

One of the greatest developmental resources we have in Duke Energy is the wealth of knowledge and experience of our people. I expect our leaders to avail themselves of that resource. I want them to talk to one another, ask questions, and share ideas. I expect them to work – and learn and grow – together.

I've seen too many talented men and women attempt to lead in isolation, distancing themselves from others, believing they must set themselves apart from the rank and file. But the best examples of leaders I've seen are those who interact with broad bases of teammates, colleagues, peers, and friends. They cast their net widely, welcoming input and ideas from all.

One final observation: Lead wherever you are. Too often we think of leadership as an end goal, a future state to which we aspire. I encourage colleagues to seize it now!

We all have opportunities to lead, and companies need leaders at all levels. We need individuals who are motivated and who motivate others, individuals who add value – increasing value – to the company and its stakeholders, individuals who make a difference, challenge the status quo, and take risks.

Don't wait for a promotion or permission to lead. Do it now. Lead projects, lead discussions, lead work teams, lead by example, by questioning, and by coaching. Leadership may not be in your job description, but I propose that it is in your destiny.

Building a Successful Team

Leadership talent is mission-critical to a company's ability to effectively execute bold strategy and achieve strong results. Success requires a commitment to building bench strength throughout the enterprise, preparing employees and leaders to shape and succeed in the brave new worlds of our industry and markets.

Duke Energy is by no means alone in our quest to recruit, develop, and maintain the best talent on the market. In today's economy, we are seeing a real war for talent, and we know that to win in our competitive field, we have to win the talent war. We have to attract, retain, and develop diverse competencies and leadership abilities.

The winners in the war for talent will be those companies whose sense of mission is great and who view talent in the live-or-die mentality of battle. Top-tier talent isn't a war trophy. It's the most basic of business survival tools.

At Duke Energy, we are clearly defining the link between individual development and contribution to business strategy. We have processes in place for determining leadership developmental needs, creating developmental plans, and identifying the core competencies to which we aspire. Recognizing that intellectual capital is our greatest asset, we have fostered a learning environment that reaffirms our business strategies and motivates employees to take on more responsibility, assume more risk, and solve complex and demanding problems.

Leadership development is just good business. Investors consider the quality of a corporation's management. Talented people prefer to work for companies that invest in development. Customers prefer to work with corporations that can solve problems and add value.

Obviously, development is first and foremost the responsibility of the individual employee. An enterprise-wide leadership initiative by no means removes that individual accountability.

The corporation cannot substitute for individual attention, self-awareness, and dedication. But the corporation can and should champion a management focus on and support of development. Infusing our employees with a clear corporate vision, with a shared commitment to continuous learning, and with competitive market, financial, and technical competencies is crucial to our success.

We need to provide an enterprise-wide knowledge base that facilitates the cross-business line collaboration and integration that underpin our strategy. We need to be open to and on the lookout for rotational and cross-business line development opportunities that add depth to our ranks.

Learning leadership occurs in many ways. It can be deliberate, intentional, and nurtured over a long cycle; other times it will be reactive and serendipitous. My goal is to increase the percentage that is deliberate, intentional, and planned and that pays off rapidly, and to minimize the elements of risk, reaction, and mismatch.

Author and futurist Alvin Toffler wrote, "The illiterate of the 21st century will not be those who cannot read and write, but those who cannot learn, unlearn, and relearn."

Duke Energy is striving for leadership literacy, and we compete on brainpower, not brawn. Even though we're bigger than ever, our success will come from great minds working together to achieve great results. We need entrepreneurial, transformational leaders, leaders who have the foresight to make the deal – and the skills the make the deal work. Aire de Geus, head of planning for Royal Dutch/Shell once said, "The ability to learn faster than your competitors may be your only sustainable competitive advantage."

The word career comes from the French word carriere, which originally meant a "racing course." As a verb, it means "to move at full speed." In today's world, careers and leadership come down to a race against change. We are faced with growing as fast and nimbly as the challenges we face in our work. The contest demands the best we have to offer personally and as a team.

We have very strong performers in our organization, who combine professional and business knowledge with commitment and enthusiasm. In our competitive environment, we need team members who come to work every morning with a spirit of constant, creative persistence. You can get knocked to your knees on some days, but you need to be able to stand up and get back in the game.

Give More than the Expected

The best piece of business advice I ever got was from a sole proprietor who owned a pool company and built in-ground pools. He hired me when I was 18 years old, and I worked for him for two summers. He had quite a large pool operation, the largest in our region, and I was on the construction team.

One day I had the chance to ask him how he had built his business. The approach he described was straightforward. He went out and looked for contacts, sold pools at a fixed price, and provided a schedule. Those factors were very important to customers. They wanted to know they could afford the pool, and they wanted to know when they'd be able to take their first swim. Once he had sold the pool, our job was to deliver. And here's the key: We needed to deliver not just on schedule, but ahead of schedule, because that created satisfaction, a tremendous intangible. Let your customer swim in the pool a week or two before they thought they'd be able to. And we had to be able to deliver that pool within that time frame for less than we expected when we went in.

My boss stressed the importance of customer service and satisfaction over and over again. That led to repeat business, from neighbors who observed the installation and from satisfied customers who called him again when they moved on to new homes. That was a simple, straightforward model of what makes a business work.

I remember saying to myself, now that I know what the company does and how it works, I can contribute in different ways. I may be on the construction crew, but I can be nice to the pool purchaser. I can make sure this product is available for them to swim in two weeks ahead of time. I can push to make sure everything is cleaned up nice and neat when we're done.

While we were building the pools, neighbors came over all the time. Since there were no sales people around, and the owner told me the neighbors were where the next five orders would come from, I thought, anywhere I can contribute, I will. The first summer I just tried to make my way, but the second summer I understood the business model, and I was working like a dog on that business model. I figured if it was successful, I'd be successful. When all was said and done, I got a bonus and a pat on the back because I had figured out what made the business succeed.

That perspective from early summer employment has stayed with me. It continues to resonate with me because the business model my boss shared applies to just about every business I've been involved in. I've been involved with airline, banking, and automotive industry boards of directors, so I've learned how those businesses run. And I continue to be struck by how that simple model really works across industries. Every business has its own nuances, but customer service, integrity, reliable execution, and competitive pricing and performance are essential elements of business success.

Balancing Life and Work

The best personal advice I've received, and the best I can offer, is to maintain a balance between life and work. That's not easy, and in most cases, it's an ability you have to learn. I have found you have to focus on understanding and valuing your priorities. Those priorities will move around as you go through the phases of your life and career, so you have to be flexible to accommodate competing demands for your time and attention.

My number one priority has always been family. Business is very demanding and consuming. If you're not careful, you'll find yourself addressing just the demands of the business. Your family can pre-empt that in a New York minute! You also need to create time and space for yourself, which I've had to work at. If you do that and do it correctly, you can create a robust and enjoyable career. If you get those things out of whack, they can wreak havoc. I've been very fortunate. I have been married for 33 years to a wonderful woman, and I have two grown children of whom I am extremely proud.

Management Style

I am extremely results-oriented and characterize myself as a practical visionary. I have a clear view of a desired destination, and I am equally focused on the route we need to take to get there – and the horsepower of our engine. I enjoy looking at strategies and focusing on the ones that will work, based on market understanding and shareholder value potential.

I'm also an integrator by nature. I tend to see patterns in data where others may see randomness, and I seek connections among our businesses, our people, our customers, and our markets. In a company as large and diverse as ours, building and maintaining the interconnections among business lines and geographic locations is challenging, but it is absolutely essential.

I also consider myself team-oriented. As my career has progressed, I've moved from the role of individual performer, which I thoroughly enjoyed, to marshalling and motivating team performance.

I have studied the science of applying resources wisely and leading teams to achieve desired results and find it immensely rewarding to focus our collective energies on achieving the highest level of performance and value creation. It is very satisfying to me when we reach the point at which we have clear understanding, throughout the organization, of our goals and tactics, when employees understand their individual roles in company success and work together in new and value-adding ways, and when we execute a plan successfully, hitting the bull's eye on the target we've set. And, when the course of the arrow teaches us something in the process, that is the greatest reward of all. If the execution of one plan leads to bigger and bolder goals, greater knowledge, and finesse, then we have achieved success for the long term.

Valuing Values

I began by talking about the constant pulse of change in business. I'll close with some observations on what won't change.

Ethical conduct is inextricably linked to Duke Energy's brand. It is not only a defining aspect of our heritage, but also key to our competitive advantage.

More than ever before, our business – and the knowledge economy in which we operate – are driven by intellectual and human capital. In this new arena, integrity, character, trust, partnership, and respect are critical success factors. We build our business by building relationships, so corporate behavior is every bit as important as corporate performance.

We want to do good business, in which all involved parties do well and achieve their objectives, and no one party bullies another. That's bad business, plain and simple. When we have found ourselves in a bad business situation, we re-negotiate, even in cases where we might have inadvertently had an advantage.

We have all seen reputations tarnished by flawed judgment and seemingly minor indiscretions. In business – government and all sectors – we are constantly reminded of the precariousness of corporate character. Carefully built and attended to over time, good reputations can be decimated by a very short fuse. And those fuses can be ignited by actual transgressions, inadvertent missteps, unfounded allegations – and even by the mere perception of impropriety.

So our responsibility extends beyond exemplary conduct to ensuring that we avoid any hint of impropriety.

We do that by steering clear of the "gray zone" – the area between what we know to be ethical conduct and what we know to be unethical. We need to bring that gray zone into sharper relief, where possible, provide tools for our folks to use when they're unsure of the boundaries, and set a standard of expectation that triggers our conscience and guides our actions.

We also need to think about the long-term implications of our everyday decisions and actions. If we ever do cross into the territory of unscrupulous business – and it only takes one employee making the wrong call – then any past decision made in the gray zone will be called into question. Once-friendly stakeholders who were inclined to give us the benefit of the doubt will be more skeptical – and we lose the invaluable business currency of trust and respect.

This isn't easy stuff. Ethical dilemmas are hard to spot at times. We often don't recognize the ethical quandary until the decision point has passed. That's another reason for giving careful, long-term deliberation to the decisions we make today. In the courts of law and public opinion, we don't have the benefit of hindsight.

Like most companies, we have a wealth of good minds and moral fortitude within Duke Energy, and no one needs to make a decision or resolve a conflict alone. I encourage our leaders to test their decisions and those of their teams, to push back, challenge decisions, and consider how decisions look from an outside vantage point.

We have a large contingent of employees who are new to Duke Energy, and so we are being more thoughtful and systematic in deploying ethical business values broadly and deeply within our organization. Our core leadership team is responsible for setting the example – and the expectation – regarding ethical conduct in our organization. One of the ways we set the example is by setting a high bar in our organization and championing this more systematic attention to ethical business conduct.

We also maintain an open-door policy that invites the exploration and hashing-out of potential ethical issues. By helping guide our teammates in making the tough judgment calls, we develop and reinforce that critical capacity and sensitivity.

There is a tendency today to view corporate America with a skeptical eye. Whether or not that skepticism is deserved, management integrity and corporate credibility will increasingly be part of the criteria for evaluating investment decisions. Shady business deals, questionable accounting, excessive promotion, and arrogant conduct can stop a company in its tracks.

I believe the contributions of business to society, both in the U.S. and worldwide, have been monumental and defining. We have energized economies, improved the standard of living, satisfied the needs and desires of generations, and helped educate and enlighten. We have much good to offer going forward, and at Duke Energy, we are dedicated to making a positive difference in the lives of our customers and in the global communities where we work.

Richard B. Priory is chairman of the board, president, and chief executive officer of Duke Energy Corporation, a leader in providing global energy services. He also serves as a member of the company's Policy Committee. He was president and chief operating officer of Duke Power Company before its merger with PanEnergy Corp in 1997.

From 1969 to 1972, Mr. Priory was a design and project engineer at Union Carbide Corporation. He served as an assistant professor of structural engineering at the University of North Carolina at Charlotte from 1973 to 1976.

A native of Lakehurst, New Jersey, Mr. Priory graduated magna cum laude from West Virginia Institute of Technology with a Bachelor of Science degree in civil engineering and received a Master of Science degree in engineering from Princeton University. He is a graduate of the University of Michigan's Public Utility Executive Program and Harvard University's Advanced Management Program. He received an honorary Doctorate of Science degree from West Virginia University Institute of Technology.

Mr. Priory was elected to membership in the National Academy of Engineering in 1993. He serves on the North Carolina Governor's Business Council of Management and Development, the Conference Board's board of trustees, the National Petroleum Council, and the Business Roundtable. He is a member of the boards of directors of several companies and the Foundation of the University of North Carolina at Charlotte, and is chairman, Charlotte Institute for Technology Innovation, University of North Carolina at Charlotte.

A member of the President's Advisory Group, the Chamber of Commerce of the United States of America, and the Business Council, Mr. Priory received the 1999 Ellis Island Medal of Honor.